WHY MARRY?

(Originally published under the title
"And So They Were Married")

BY
JESSE LYNCH WILLIAMS

ILLUSTRATED

COPYRIGHT, 1914, 1918, BY
CHARLES SCRIBNER'S SONS

Published October, 1914
New and revised edition published April, 1918
Reprinted September, 1918; *February,* 1919

[All rights strictly reserved—including amateur acting rights.]

Printing Statement:

Due to the very old age and scarcity of this book, many of the pages may be hard to read due to the blurring of the original text, possible missing pages, missing text, dark backgrounds and other issues beyond our control.

Because this is such an important and rare work, we believe it is best to reproduce this book regardless of its original condition.

Thank you for your understanding.

TO
HARRIET AND JAMES LEES LAIDLAW

WHY MARRY?
A Comedy in Three Acts

New York: Astor Theatre: Produced by Selwyn & Company, Dec. 25, 1917, under the direction of Roi Cooper Megrue.

The scene is a week-end at a country house not far away; the time, Saturday afternoon, Sunday morning, and Sunday evening.

THE PEOPLE AT THE HOUSE
(As You Meet Them)

JEAN, the host's younger sister, who has been brought up to be married and nothing else..............LOTUS ROBB

REX, an unmarried neighbor, who has not been brought up to be anything but rich..................HAROLD WEST

LUCY, the hostess, who is trying her best to be "just an old-fashioned wife" in a new-fashioned home,
BEATRICE BECKLEY

UNCLE EVERETT, a Judge, who belongs to the older generation and yet understands the new—and believes in divorce.........................NAT C. GOODWIN

COUSIN THEODORE, a clergyman and yet a human being, who believes in everything—except divorce,
ERNEST LAWFORD

JOHN, who owns the house and almost every one in it—and does not believe in divorce.........EDMUND BREESE

HELEN, the host's other sister, whom every one wants to marry, but who doesn't want to marry any one,
ESTELLE WINWOOD

ERNEST, a scientist, who believes in neither divorce nor marriage but makes a great discovery...SHELLEY HULL
(By arrangement with George C. Tyler)

THE BUTLER....................RICHARD PITMAN

THE FOOTMAN...................WALTER GOODSON

ADVANCE NOTICE
BY THE AUTHOR

One afternoon shortly before the New York "opening" of this comedy a most estimable lady sat down to make me a cup of tea.

"Now, do tell me, what is your play about?" she inquired with commendable enthusiasm. For, being a true woman, she had early achieved the becoming habit of letting members of the superior sex talk about themselves.

"'Why Marry?'" said I, "tells the truth about marriage."

"Oh, why," she expostulated, "why write unpleasant plays?"

"But it is not 'unpleasant.'"

"Then it isn't true!" she exclaimed. "That is, I mean—I mean—did you say cream or lemon?"

And in the pause which accompanied the pouring of the cream I detected the look of one realizing too late that it is always better to think before speaking.

This little incident, it seemed to me, epitomizes charmingly the attitude of "our nicest people" toward our fundamental institution. The truth about marriage must be unpleasant.

Advance Notice

Therefore, tell us something we know isn't true. It will be so much nicer for our young people.

It is to be feared, however, that young people who go to see "Why Marry?" in the hope of being shocked do not get their money's worth. I have heard of but two persons who have been scandalized by this play, and they were both old people. One was a woman in the country who had not seen it, but had read the title, and so wrote several indignant letters about it. The other was an elderly bachelor of the type which finds useful occupation in decorating club windows like geraniums. He took his niece to see it, and, deciding at the end of Act II that the play was going to be unpleasant in Act III, took her home at once. The next afternoon she appeared at the matinée with a whole bevy of her own generation and saw the rest of the play. I asked her later if it had shocked any of them.

"Oh, no," she replied, "we are too young to be shocked."

That little incident also struck me as socially significant. There never were two generations inhabiting the same globe simultaneously with such widely separated points of view.

For several years after this play was first published no theatrical manager on Broadway would

Advance Notice

produce it. I don't blame them, I want to thank them for it. I doubt if this sort of thing could have appealed to many theatre-goers then, especially as my young lovers are trying to be good, not bad. "Self-expression" and "the right to happiness" do not enter into their plans. The causes of their courageous and, of course, mistaken decision are unselfish and social motives, however futile and antisocial the results would have been had not their desperate determination been thwarted. . . . When this play was first published most people were not thinking along these lines. Such ideas were considered radical then. They will soon be old-fashioned—even on the stage.

Kind and discriminating as the critics have been in regard to this comedy (a discriminating critic being, of course, one who praises your play), few of them have seen the point which I thought I was making emphatically clear, namely, that we can't cure social defects by individual treatment. Not only the lovers, but all the characters in this play are trying to do right according to their lights. There is no villain in this piece. At least the villain remains "off stage." Perhaps that is why so few see him. You are the villain, you and I and the rest of society. We are responsible for the rules and regulations

Advance Notice

of the marriage game. Instead of having fun with human nature, I tried to go higher up and have fun with human institutions.

I say "tried," because apparently I did not succeed. The joke is on me. Still, I can get some amusement out of it: for a great many people seem to like this play who would be indignant if they knew what they were really applauding. They think they are merely enjoying "satire on human nature." Now, it is a curious fact that you can always curse human nature with impunity; can malign it, revile it, boot it up and down the decalogue, and you will be warmly praised. "How true to life!" you are told. "I know some one just like that." (It is always some one else, of course.) But dare lay hands on the Existing Order—and you'll find you've laid your hands on a hornet's nest.

You see, most people do not want anything changed—except possibly the Law of Change. They do not object to finding fault with mankind because "you can't change human nature," as they are fond of telling you with an interesting air of originality. But laws, customs, and ideals can be changed, can be improved. Therefore they cry: "Hands off! How dare you!" Man made human institutions, therefore we reverence them. Whereas human nature was merely made

Advance Notice

by God. So we don't think so much of it. We are prejudiced, like all creators, in favor of our own creations. After all, there is excellent precedent for such complacency. Even God, we are informed, pronounced his work "all very good" and rested on the seventh day.

Pretty nearly everything in the play as acted is in the book as published; but by no means all that is in the book could possibly be enacted on the stage in two hours and a half. One scene, a breakfast scene between John and his wife, has been amplified for acting, but all the other scenes as printed here have been shortened for stage purposes and one or two cut out entirely.

The "set" was changed to represent the loggia, instead of the terrace, of John's "little farm." Outdoor scenes are not supposed to be good for comedy. Walls, or a suggestion of them, produce a better psychological effect for the purpose, besides making it possible to speak in quieter, more intimate tones than when the voice spills out into the wings and up into the paint loft.

Near the end of the play a number of relatives, rich and poor, are supposed to arrive for dinner and for influencing by their presence the recalcitrant couple. That is the way it is printed

Advance Notice

and that is how it was acted during the first few weeks of the Chicago run. But though the family may have its place in the book, it proved to be an awful nuisance on the stage. No matter how well these minor parts might be acted (or dressed), their sudden irruption during the last and most important moments of the performance distracted the audience's attention from the principal characters and the main issue. It was not clear who was who. Programmes fluttered; perplexity was observed. . . . So we decided that the family must be destroyed. It is always a perplexing problem to devise a substitute for the family.

Jesse Lynch Williams.

Act I

"And So They Were Married"

Act I

Up from the fragrant garden comes a girl, running. She takes the broad terrace steps two at a stride, laughing, breathless, fleet as a fawn, sweet as a rose. She is hotly pursued by a boy, handsome, ardent, attractively selfish, and just now blindly determined to catch the pretty creature before she gains the protecting shelter of home. She is determined to let him but not to let him know it. . . . There, she might have darted in through the open door, but it is such a cold, formal entrance; she pretends to be exhausted, dodges behind a stone tea-table, and, turning, faces him, each panting and laughing excitedly; she alluring and defiant, he merry and dominant.

She is twenty-five and he is a year or two older, but they are both children; in other words, unmarried.

"And So They Were Married"

Rex

Think I'll let you say that to me?

Jean
[*making a face at him*]
Think I'm afraid of you!

Rex
Take it back, I tell you.

Jean
I won't.

Rex
I'll make you.

Jean
[*with a dance step*]
Think so, do you?

Rex
I warn you.

Jean
Booh-woo!
[*He makes a feint to the right, then dashes to the left and catches her.*

"And So They Were Married"

REX
[*triumphantly*]
Now! . . . You would, would you?

JEAN
[*struggling*]
Let me go.

REX
I couldn't think of it.

JEAN
[*seizes his hands to free herself — can't*]
You're so strong — it isn't fair.

REX
You're so sweet — it isn't fair.
[*Smiling down at her struggles, rejoicing in his strength, her weakness, he gently draws her near.*]

JEAN
[*knows what is coming*]
No, Rex.

REX
Yes.

"And So They Were Married"

JEAN
You mustn't.

REX
But I will.

[*He laughs and kisses her lightly on the cheek. Therefore she struggles furiously. Therefore he does it again. And again. Suddenly he enfolds her completely and kisses her passionately — cheeks, mouth, eyes — until she gasps in alarm. Laughter has gone from them now.*

JEAN
Oh, please! . . . some one will come.

REX
[*with the intoxication of such moments*]
I don't care who comes — I love you.

JEAN
No . . . let me go.

REX
Not till you kiss me, Jean. [JEAN *hesitates, brushes his cheek lightly with her lips, and in pretty confusion tries to escape.*] Not till you

"And So They Were Married"

say you love me, Jean. [*Eyes hidden in his coat, she bobs her head. He laughs and loves it.*] Say it!

JEAN

I — er — do.

REX

Do *what?* . . . Say it! . . .

    [*She cannot. He swings her about, bringing her face close to his.*

JEAN

I love you, Rex. Are you sure you love me?

REX

Am I sure! You irresistible little —
    [*Begins to kiss her. Masculine triumph.*

JEAN

And want to marry me, Rex?

REX

[*stops — startled — had not thought of that*]
Why — er — of course. What did you suppose!
    [*Drops his eyes, sobered.*

"And So They Were Married"

JEAN
[*feminine triumph*]
And me "a penniless orphing"?

REX
[*fascinated by the way she says it, he laughs. Then, his honor touched*]
Why, what kind of a man do you take me for!
[*And wants her lips again.*

JEAN
[*giving herself to him, head sinks upon his shoulder*]
Then, oh, Rex, love me and be nice to me and — and take me away from all this!

> [*She covers her face with her hands and sobs. He pats her tenderly, with a manly look on his face.*
> LUCY *comes up from the garden. She is dressed in white with a garden hat, a garden basket filled with flowers in one hand, long scissors in the other. She is* JOHN'S *wife, the mistress of the house, sister-in-law to* JEAN; *conspicuously a "sweet" woman, affectedly so, a contrast with* JEAN'S *more modern, less delicate charm.* JEAN *is frank*

"And So They Were Married"

and brave, Lucy *indirect and timid, pretty but fading, forty but fighting it.*

Jean
[*laughing*]
It's all right, Lucy — we're engaged!

Lucy
Well, I should hope so!
[*Shoots a look at* Jean, "*So?*"]

Rex
[*recovering himself*]
I have often tried to thank you and good old John for letting me come over here so much, but now! How can I *ever* thank you? See-what-I-mean?

Lucy
I'll tell you how. Behave yourself after you are married to John's little sister.

Jean
Rex, have you had a fearful past? How fascinating!

"And So They Were Married"

Rex

I'm going to have a glorious future, all right.

Jean

Not unless you do as I tell you. Going to obey me, Rex?

Rex

You bet I am.

Jean

Then begin now. Go! . . . Get out! [*She pushes* Rex, *laughing and protesting, toward the garden.*] I want to tell Lucy how nice you are. Run along over to the golf club, and by and by — if you *are* a good boy — you can take me out in your new car. [Rex *kisses the hand on his arm and leaves, laughing.*] My dear, he has five cars! Thank you so much.

[*Alone, they throw off the mask worn before men.*

Lucy

Now, deary, tell me all about it. How did it happen?

Jean

Oh, I simply followed your advice.

"And So They Were Married"

Lucy
Picked a quarrel with him?

Jean
[*laughing*]
Yes. I pretended to believe in woman suffrage!

Lucy
Good! They hate that.

Jean
I told him all men were bullying brutes!

Lucy
They are! And then you ran away?

Jean
Of course.

Lucy
And he after you?

Jean
Of course.

Lucy
And you let him catch you?

"And So They Were Married"

Jean

Of cour — well . . . he caught me.

[*They both laugh.*

Lucy

I can guess the rest.

Jean

Why, it didn't take five minutes.

Lucy

And now it's to last through all eternity. . . . Isn't love wonderful?

Jean

Um-hum. Wonderful.

[*They begin to cull out the flowers.*

Lucy

But you do love him, dear, don't you?

Jean

[*arranging flowers*]

I did then. I don't now. Why is that, Lucy?

Lucy

Oh, but you will learn to love him. [*Jean shrugs, drops flowers, and turns away.*] Now,

"And So They Were Married"

now! no worrying — it brings wrinkles! [*Patting* Jean's *shoulder.*] Rex is just the sort to give the woman he adores everything in the world.

Jean
[*wriggling out of* Lucy's *embrace*]
I am not the woman he adores.

Lucy
Why, Jean! He's engaged to you.

Jean
But he's in love with my sister. You know that as well as I do.

Lucy
[*uncomfortably*]
Oh, well, he was once, but not now. Men admire these independent women, but they don't marry them. Nobody wants to marry a sexless freak with a scientific degree.

Jean
Oh, what's the use, Lucy? He's still wild about Helen, and she still laughs at him. So you and John have trotted out the little sister. Why not be honest about it.

"And So They Were Married"

Lucy

Well, I may be old-fashioned, but I don't think it's nice to talk this way when you're just engaged.

Jean

Here comes your "sexless freak"—not with a degree, either.

Lucy
[*following* Jean's *gaze*]

With a man!

Jean
[*smiling*]

With *my* man.

[Helen, *with* Rex *bending toward her eagerly, appears. She is a beautiful woman of twenty-nine, tall, strong, glorious—plenty of old-fashioned charm, despite her new-fashioned ideas. She is dressed in a tennis costume and is swinging a racquet.*

Rex

But they told me you were going to stay abroad all winter.

"And So They Were Married"

Helen
My work, Rex — I had to get back to work.

Rex
Work! . . . You are too good to work.

Jean
[*amused, not jealous*]
Is this your high-powered car, Rex? Have you learned to run it yet?

Rex
[*startled*]
But . . . well . . . you see, I met Helen on the way. See-what-I-mean?

Jean
[*laughing*]
Oh, we see.

Rex
But I hadn't seen her for so long. I thought — [*Looks from* Helen *to* Jean] . . . wait, I'll get the car.   [*He hurries off.*

Lucy
[*to* Jean]
Why couldn't she have stayed abroad!

"And So They Were Married"

JEAN

Helen, don't talk about your work before Lucy — it shocks her.

HELEN

Oh, very well; make it my 'career'!

JEAN
[*arm around* HELEN]

Sssh! — that's worse.

LUCY

Helen, dear, I deem it my duty to tell you that you are being talked about.

HELEN

Lucy, dear, do you always find your true happiness in duty?

LUCY

Well, if you think you are going back to that horrid place again . . . after what happened that night? John won't hear of it.

HELEN

If the Baker Institute of Medical Experiment is not a respectable place you should make John resign as trustee. [*She laughs it off.*

"And So They Were Married"

Lucy

John is trustee of — oh, nearly everything. That makes it all the worse. It isn't as if you had to work.

Helen

Oh, but John is so rich now, his credit can stand it. And you oughtn't to mind! Why, some of our most fashionable families now contain freaks like me. It's becoming quite smart, just as in former days one of the sons would go into the Church or the navy.

Lucy

Well, of course, I am old-fashioned, but going down-town every day with the men, — it seems so unwomanly.

Helen

But wasn't I womanly for years? Instead of going down-town and working with highbrows, I stayed up-town and played with lowbrows — until I was bored to death.

Lucy
[*sighs*]

Yes, that's what comes of going to college, leaving the home, getting these new ideas. All

"And So They Were Married"

the same, Helen, the men, really nice men, don't like it.

Helen

Well, you see, I don't like really nice men, so that makes it agreeable all around.

Lucy

If it were only art or music or something feminine, but that awful laboratory! How can a lady poison poor, innocent little monkeys?

Helen

If I were a lady I'd *dine* with monkeys. . . . Do you know what the word means, Lucy? In Anglo-Saxon times "lady" meant "one who gives loaves"; now, one who *takes* a loaf.

Lucy

Very clever, my dear, but some day you'll be sorry. No man, Helen, likes a woman to have independent views.

Jean

Helen can afford to have independent views; she has an independent income — she earns it.

"And So They Were Married"

Lucy

Independent income! Her salary wouldn't pay for your hats.

Jean

All the same, I wish I had gone to college; I wish I had learned a profession.

Lucy

What have these New Women accomplished? Just one thing: they are destroying chivalry!

Helen

Not entirely, Lucy, not entirely. For instance, I am the best assistant Ernest Hamilton has, but the worst paid; the others are all men. Hurray for chivalry!

Lucy

Well, I'm just an old-fashioned wife. Woman's sphere is the home. My husband says so.

Helen

But suppose you haven't any husband! What can a spinster do in the home?

Lucy

Stay in it — till she gets one! That's what the old-fashioned spinster used to do.

"And So They Were Married"

Helen

The old-fashioned spinster used to spin.

Lucy

At any rate, the old-fashioned spinster did not stay out of her home all night and get herself compromised, talked about, sent abroad! Or, if she did, she knew enough to remain abroad until the gossip blew over. [*Lucy turns to leave.*

Helen

[*mischievously*]

Ah, that wonderful night! [Lucy *turns back, amazed.*] The night we discovered the Hamilton antitoxin, the night that made the Baker Institute famous! And, just think, I had a hand in it, Lucy, a hand in the unwomanly work of saving children's lives! But, of course, an old-fashioned spinster would have blushed and said: "Excuse me, Doctor Hamilton, but we must now let a year's work go to waste because you are a man and I am a woman, and it's dark outdoors!" . . . That's the way to preserve true chivalry.

Lucy

You think we can't see through all this? Science — fiddlesticks! The good-looking young

"And So They Were Married"

scientist — that's why you couldn't stay abroad. We see it, John sees it, and now every one will see it. Then how will you feel?

Helen

Ernest *is* rather good-looking, isn't he?

Lucy

Do you think your brother will let you marry a mere scientist! . . . Oh, well, Doctor Hamilton is in love with his work — fortunately. . . . Besides, he's a thoroughbred; he wouldn't even look at a girl who throws herself at his head.

Helen

So I needn't try any longer? Too bad.

Lucy

[losing her temper and going]

Oh, you New Women are quite superior, aren't you? . . . Thank heavens, little Jean didn't elbow *her* way into men's affairs; she had no unwomanly ambitions for a career! But she is engaged to Rex Baker!

Helen

Jean, is this true?

"And So They Were Married"

Lucy
[*triumphantly*]

Marriage is woman's only true career.

Helen

Jean! You can't, you won't, you mustn't marry Rex!

Lucy
[*flouncing out*]

"She who will not when she may," my dear!

Jean
[*avoiding* Helen's *eyes*]

Lucy hears John coming — he'd take her head off if she weren't there to meet him. [Helen *only looks at her.*] He bullies and browbeats her worse than ever. I can't stand it here much longer. It's getting on my nerves.

Helen

Jean! You care for Rex no more than I do.

Jean
[*still evasive*]

John's bringing out Uncle Everett and Cousin Theodore. My dear, the whole family is up in the air about you.

"And So They Were Married"

Helen

Oh, I can take care of myself, but you! . . . Jean, you're not the sort to marry Rex or any other man, unless you simply can't live without him.

Jean

[*after a little pause*]

Well . . . how can I live without him — without some man? You can support yourself. I can't.

Helen

But you wouldn't live on a man you didn't really love!

Jean

Why not? Lucy does; most wives live on men they don't really love. To stop doing so and get divorced is wrong, you know.

Helen

Jean, Jean, poor little Jean!

Jean

Well, I'd rather have domestic unhappiness of my own than watch other people's all my life.

"And So They Were Married"

Helen

I don't like to hurt you, dear, but — [*Takes* Jean's *face and raises it.*] How about that nice boy at the Harvard Law School?

Jean

Don't! [*Controls herself, then, in a low voice*] Bob is *still* at the Law School, Helen.

Helen

Can't you wait, dear?

Jean

He never asked me to, Helen.

Helen

He would, if you let him.

Jean

It wouldn't be fair. It takes so long to get started. Everything costs so much. Why, nowadays, men in the professions, unless they have private means, can't marry until nearly *forty*. When Bob is forty I'll be forty, Helen.

Helen

Ah, but when a girl really cares!

"And So They Were Married"

JEAN
Helen, do *you* know?

HELEN
Never mind about me — you!

JEAN
Oh, we'll get over it, I suppose. . . . People do! Some day, perhaps, he'll smile and say: "Just think, I once loved *that* fat old thing!" [*Suddenly changes to sobbing.*] Helen! when Rex caught me and kissed me I shut my eyes and tried to think it was Bob.

HELEN
[*takes* JEAN *in her arms*]
You can't keep on thinking so, dear.

JEAN
But that isn't the worst! When he held me fast and I couldn't get away, I began . . . to forget Bob . . . to forget everything . . . [*Breaks off, overcome with shame.*] But not now, not now! It's not the same thing at all. [*Buries face in* HELEN'S *breast and sobs it out.*] Oh, I feel like the devil, dear. . . . And all this time

"And So They Were Married"

he doesn't really want me — he wants you, you! I trapped him into it; I trapped him!

HELEN

And I know Rex — he's a good sport; he'll stick to it, if you do, dear — only you won't! You've caught him by playing on his worst — don't hold him by playing on his best!

JEAN

But what shall I do? I'm nearly twenty-six. I've got to escape from home in some way.

HELEN

But what a way! [REX *returns.*

REX

Ready, Jean? [*To* HELEN.] Lucy and John and your Cousin Theodore are in there having a fine, old-fashioned family fight with the judge.

HELEN

With Uncle Everett? What about?

REX

They shut up when they saw me. All I heard

"And So They Were Married"

was the parson — "Marriage is a social institution." Grand old row, though. [*A* BUTLER *and* FOOTMAN *appear, wheeling a tea-wagon.*] Looks as if they were coming out here.

HELEN

Then I am going in. [*Detaining* JEAN.] You will follow my advice?

JEAN
[*apart to* HELEN]

Oh, I don't know. Soon or late I must follow the only profession I have learned.

> [JEAN *leaves with* REX. HELEN *watches them, sighs, and goes in. The* SERVANTS *arrange the tea-table and go into the house.*
> LUCY *comes out, followed by her husband,* JOHN, *and the* JUDGE, *who is* UNCLE EVERETT, *and* COUSIN THEODORE.
> JOHN, *the masterful type of successful American business man; well set up, close-cropped mustache, inclined to baldness; keen eye, vibrant voice, quick movements, quick decisions, quick temper.*
> UNCLE EVERETT *is a genial satirist with a*

cynical tolerance of the ways of the world, which he understands, laughs at, and rather likes.

Cousin Theodore, *a care-worn rector, who, though he buttons his collar behind, likes those who don't; a noble soul, self-sacrificing and sanctified, but he does not obtrude his profession upon others — never talks shop unless asked to do so, and prides himself upon not being a bigot.*

They are continuing an earnest discussion, with the intimate manner of friendly members of the same family. John, Lucy, *and* Theodore *deeply concerned;* Uncle Everett *detached and amused.*

Theodore

But, Uncle Everett, hasn't Aunt Julia always been a good wife to you?

Judge

Quite so, quite so, a good wife, Theodore, a good wife.

Lucy

And a *devoted* mother to your children, Uncle Everett?

"And So They Were Married"

JUDGE
Devoted, Lucy, devoted.

JOHN
She has always obeyed you, Uncle Everett.

JUDGE
Yes, John — a true, old-fashioned woman.

THEODORE
She has been a great help to me in the parish work, Uncle Everett.

JUDGE
An earnest worker in the vineyard, Theodore — in fact, I might say, a model female.

ALL
Then why, *why* do you want a divorce?

JUDGE
Because, damn it, I don't like her!

LUCY
But think of poor Aunt Julia!

"And So They Were Married"

JUDGE

But, damn it, she doesn't like *me*.

THEODORE
[*wagging head sadly*]

Ah, yes, I suppose there has been fault on both sides.

JUDGE

Not at all! No fault on either side. . . . Both patterns of Christian fortitude to the end! We still are. Just listen to this telegram.

LUCY
[*puzzled*]

From Aunt Julia?

JUDGE

Yes from Aunt Julia in Reno. Not used to travelling without me; knew I'd worry. Thoughtful of her, wasn't it? [*Puts on glasses.*] A night letter. Much cheaper; your Aunt Julia was always a frugal wife. Besides, she never could keep within ten words. [*Reads.*] "Arrived safely. Charming rooms with plenty of air and sunlight. Our case docketed for March 15th. Wish you were here to see the women in

"And So They Were Married"

Divorcee Row — overdressed and underbred." Rather neat, eh? "Overdressed and underbred." "I should love to hear *your* comments on the various types." Now, isn't that sweet of her? Well, you know, I always *could* make her laugh — except when I made her cry. "Write soon. With love. Julia." Now [*folds telegram*], isn't that a nice message? From a wife suing for divorce? You happily married people couldn't beat that. [*Pats telegram and pockets it tenderly.*

John
[*like a practical business man*]

But if there's no other woman, no other man — what's it all about?

Judge

She likes her beefsteak well done; I like mine underdone. She likes one window open — about so much [*indicates four inches*]; I like all the windows open wide! She likes to stay at home; I like to travel. She loves the opera and hates the theatre; I love the theatre and hate the opera.

Theodore

Stop! aren't you willing to make a few little sacrifices for each other? Haven't you character enough for that?

"And So They Were Married"

Judge

We've been making sacrifices for twenty-five years, a quarter of a century! Character enough to last us now . . . Why, I remember the first dinner we had together after we were pronounced man and wife, with a full choral service and a great many expensive flowers — quite a smart wedding, Lucy, for those simple days. "Darling," I asked my blushing bride, "do you like tutti-frutti ice-cream?" "I adore it, dearest," she murmured. I hated it, but nobly sacrificed myself and gave her tutti-frutti and gained character every evening of our honeymoon! Then when we got back and began our "new life" together in our "little home," my darling gave *me* tutti-frutti and indigestion *once a week* until I nearly died!

Lucy

But why didn't you tell her?

Judge

I did; I did. Got chronic dyspepsia and struck! "*You* may adore this stuff, *darling*," I said, "but I hate it." "So do I, dearest," says she. "Then why in thunder have you had it all

"And So They Were Married"

these years, *sweetheart?*" "For your sake, *beloved!*" And that tells the whole story of our married life. We have nothing in common but a love of divorce and a mutual abhorrence of tutti-frutti. "Two souls with but a single thought, two hearts that beat as one!" It has been the dream of our lives to get apart, and each has nobly refrained for the other's sake. And all in vain!

John

Bah! All a cloak to hide his real motive. And he knows it!

Judge
[*after a painful pause*]

I may as well confess. [*Looks around to see if overheard. Whispers.*] For over twenty years I — I have broken my marriage vow! [Lucy *drops her eyes.* Theodore *aghast.* John *wags head.*] So has your Aunt Julia!

Theodore

No! not that!

Judge

Well, we solemnly promised to love each other until death did us part. We have broken

"And So They Were Married"

that sacred vow! I don't love *her;* she doesn't love *me* — not in the least!

John

Rot! A matured, middle-aged man, a distinguished member of the bar — break up his home for that? Damned rot!

Judge

Right again, John. That's not why I'm breaking up my home. I prefer my club. What does the modern home amount to? Merely a place to leave your wife.

Lucy

Of course, it doesn't matter about the poor little wife left at home.

Judge

Wrong, Lucy, it does matter. That's why I *stayed* at home and was bored to death with her prattle about clothes and the opera, instead of dining at the club with my intellectual equals, picking up business there, getting rich like John, supplying her with *more* clothes and a whole *box* at the opera, like yours, Lucy.

"And So They Were Married"

Lucy
[*shoots a glance at her husband*]
Oh, that's the way you men *always* talk. It never occurs to you that business, business, *business* is *just* as much of a bore to us!

Judge
Wrong again! It did occur to *me* — hence the divorce! She couldn't stand seeing *me* bored; I couldn't stand seeing *her* bored. Once we could deceive each other; but now — too well acquainted; our happy home — a hollow mockery!

Theodore
You ought to be ashamed! I love my home!

John
So do I. [*He glances sternly at* Lucy.

Lucy
[*nervously*]
So do I.

Judge
All right. Stick to it, if you love it. Only, don't claim credit for doing what you enjoy.

"And So They Were Married"

I stuck to my home for a quarter of a century and disliked it the whole time. At last I'm free to say so. Just think of it, Lucy, free to utter those things about marriage we all know are true but don't dare say! Free to be honest, John! No longer a hypocrite, no longer a liar! A soul set free, Theodore — two souls, in fact. "Two souls with but a single thought ——"

Theodore

Stop! You have *children* to consider, not merely your own selfish happiness!

Lucy

Yes, think of Tom and little Julia!

Judge

We did . . . for a quarter of a century — sacrificed everything to them, even our self-respect; but now — what's the use? We are childless now. Tom and Julia have both left us for "little homes" of their own to love.

Theodore

Ah, but don't you want them to have the old home to come back to?

"And So They Were Married"

JUDGE

"No place like home" for children, eh? You're right — can't have too much of it. Most children only have *one* home. Ours will have *two!* When they get bored with one they can try the other.

THEODORE

But, seriously, Uncle Everett — "Whom God hath joined together!"

LUCY

[*clasping* JOHN'S *arm*]

Yes, Uncle Everett, marriages are made in heaven.

JUDGE

I see; quite so; but your Aunt Julia and I were joined together by a pink parasol made in Paris.

JOHN

What rot! Stop your fooling and speak the truth, man.

JUDGE

Just what I'm doing — that's why you think I'm fooling. A very pretty parasol — but it wasn't made in heaven. You see, God made poor,

"And So They Were Married"

dear Julia pale, but on that fatal day, twenty-five years ago, the pink parasol, not God, made her rosy and irresistible. I did the rest — with the aid of a clergyman, whom I tipped even more liberally than the waiter who served us tutti-frutti. Blame *me* for it, blame her, the parasol, the parson, but do not, my dear Theodore, blame the Deity for our own mistakes. It's so blasphemous.

[*A pause.* LUCY *takes place at the tea-table to serve tea.*

LUCY

And to think we invited *you*, of all people, here to-day of all days! [*To* JOHN.] We mustn't let Rex know. The Bakers don't believe in divorce.

JOHN

What's this? You don't mean that Jean——?

LUCY

Yes! Just in time — before he knew Helen was back.

JOHN

[*jumps up*]

She's landed him! She's landed him! We're marrying into the Baker family! The Baker

"And So They Were Married"

family! [*Shaking hands right and left.*] Why, she'll have more money than any of us! . . . Well, well! We'll all have to stand around before little Jean now! . . . My, my! Lucy, you're a wonder! Those pearls — I'll buy them; they're yours! Hurray for Lucy!   [*Kisses* Lucy.

Lucy
[*feeling her importance*]

Now, if I could only get *Helen* out of this awful mess and safely married to some nice man!

Judge
[*sipping his tea*]

Meaning one having money?

Theodore

The Hamiltons are an older family than the Bakers, Lucy, older than our own.

Judge

Meaning they *once* had money.

John
[*still pacing to and fro*]

Waste a beauty on a bacteriologist? A crime!

"And So They Were Married"

Theodore

See here, John, Ernest Hamilton is the biggest thing you've got in the Baker Institute! One of the loveliest fellows in the world, too, and if you expect me — why did you ask us here, anyway?

Judge

Far as I can make out, we're here to help one of John's sisters marry a man she doesn't love and prevent the other from marrying the man she does.

John

Oh, look here: I've nothing against young Hamilton. . . . I *like* him — proud of all he's done for the institute. Why, Mr. Baker is tickled to death about the Hamilton antitoxin. But, Theodore, this is a practical world. Your scientific friend gets just two thousand dollars a year! . . . Lucy, send for Helen.

[Lucy *goes obediently.*

Judge

Well, why not give the young man a raise?

John

Oh, that's not a bad salary for scientists, college professors, and that sort of thing. Why,

"And So They Were Married"

even the head of the institute himself gets less than the superintendent of my mills. No future in science.

Judge

Perfectly practical, Theodore. The superintendent of John's mills saves the company thousands of dollars. These bacteriologists merely save the nation thousands of babies. All our laws, written and unwritten, value private property above human life. I'm a distinguished jurist and I always render my decisions accordingly. I'd be reversed by the United States Supreme Court if I didn't. We're all rewarded in inverse ratio to our usefulness to society, Theodore. That's why "practical men" think changes are "dangerous."

John

Muck-raker!

Judge

It's all on a sliding scale, John. For keeping up the cost of living you and old man Baker get . . . [*Stretches arms out full length.*] Heaven only knows how much. For saving the Constitution I get . . . a good deal. [*Hands three*

"And So They Were Married"

feet apart.] For saving in wages and operating expenses your superintendent gets so much. [*Hands two feet apart.*] For saving human life Ernest Hamilton gets that. [*Hands six inches apart.*] For saving immortal souls Theodore gets — [*Holds up two forefingers an inch apart.*] Now, if any one came along and saved the world ——

Theodore
[*interrupts*]

They crucified Him.

John

Muck-raker, muck-raker.

Lucy
[*returning*]

Tried my best, John, but Helen says she prefers to talk with you alone some time.

John
[*furious*]

She "prefers"? See here! Am I master in my own house or not?

Judge

But Helen is a guest in it now. No longer

"And So They Were Married"

under your control, John. She's the New Woman.

Theodore

John, *you* can't stop that girl's marrying Ernest, if she wants to; he's head over heels in love with her.

Lucy

What! We thought he was in love with his work!

Theodore

He thinks there's no hope for him, poor boy.

Lucy
[*to* John]

And she is mad about him!

John
[*to* Lucy]

And he is on the way out here now!

Theodore

What! He's coming to see her?

John

No, no, thinks she's still in Paris — so she was when I invited him, damn it — but some-

"And So They Were Married"

thing had to be done and done delicately. That's why I invited you two.

Judge
[*bursts out laughing*]

Beautiful! These lovers haven't met for a month, and to-night there's a moon!

Theodore
[*also laughs*]

You may as well give in, John. It's the simplest solution.

Lucy
[*timidly*]

Yes, John, she's nearly thirty, and think how she treats all the *nice* men.

John

Who's doing this? You go tell Helen . . . that her Uncle Everett wants to see her!

> [*Lucy shrugs, starts reluctantly, and lingers listening.*]

Theodore

Now, uncle, you have more influence over her than any of us — don't let her know about . . . Aunt Julia. Helen thinks the world of you.

"And So They Were Married"

Judge

Of course not, never let the rising generation suspect the truth about marriage — if you want 'em to marry.

Theodore

There are other truths than unpleasant truths, Uncle Everett, other marriages than unhappy marriages.

Judge

Want me to tell her the truth about your marriage?

Lucy
[*at the door*]

Why uncle! Even *you* must admit that Theodore and Mary are happy.

[John *is too much surprised to notice* Lucy's *presence.*

Judge

Happy? What's that got to do with it? Marriage is a social institution. Theodore said so. . . . Every time a boy kisses a girl she should first inquire: "A sacrifice for society?" And if he says, "I want to gain character, sweetheart," then — "Darling, do your duty!" and he'll do it.

Lucy

Well, Theodore has certainly done *his* duty by society — six children!

Judge

Then society hasn't done its duty by Theodore — only one salary!

John

The more credit to him! He and Mary have sacrificed everything to their children and the Church — even health!

Theodore

We don't need your pity! We don't want your praise! Poverty, suffering, even separation, have only drawn us closer together. We love each other through it all! Why, in the last letter the doctor let her write she said, she said — [*Suddenly overcome with emotion, turns abruptly.*] If you'll excuse me, Lucy . . . Sanitarium . . . the telephone.

[T HEODORE *goes into the house.*

"And So They Were Married"

JUDGE

Not praise or pity but something more substantial and, by George, I'll get it for them!

[*Turns to* JOHN, *who interrupts.*

JOHN

See the example *he* sets to society — I honor him for it.

JUDGE

Fine! but that doesn't seem to restore Mary's radiant health, Theodore's brilliant youth.

LUCY

Ah, but they have their *children* — think how they adore those beautiful children!

JUDGE

No, don't think how they adore them, think how they *rear* those beautiful children — in the streets; one little daughter dead from contagion; one son going to the devil from other things picked up in the street! If marriage is a social institution, look at it socially. Why, a marriage like mine is worth a dozen like theirs — to Society. Look at my well-launched children; look at my useful career, as a jackal to

"And So They Were Married"

Big Business; look at my now perfectly contented spouse!

Lucy

But if you are divorced!

Judge

Is the object of marriage merely to stay married?

Lucy

But character, think of the character they have gained.

Judge

Oh, is it to gain character at the expense of helpless offspring? Society doesn't gain by that — it loses, Lucy, it loses. . . . But simply because, God bless 'em, "they love each other through it all," you sentimental standpatters believe in lying about it, do you?

John
[*bored, whips out pocket check-book and fountain pen*]

Oh, talk, talk, talk! Money talks for *me*. . . . But they're both so confoundedly proud!

"And So They Were Married"

JUDGE

Go on, write that check! [JOHN *writes*.] They must sacrifice their pride, John. Nothing else left to sacrifice, I'm afraid.

JOHN

Well, you get this to them somehow.

[*Hands check to* JUDGE.

JUDGE

Aha! Talk did it. . . . Five thousand? Generous John!

JOHN

[*impatiently*]

Never mind about me. *That* problem is all settled; now about Helen. . . . Lucy! I thought I told you ——

[LUCY, *in a guilty hurry, escapes into the house.*

JUDGE

John, charity never settles problems; it perpetuates them. You can't cure social defects by individual treatment.

JOHN

[*more impatiently*]

Does talk settle anything?

"And So They Were Married"

Judge

Everything. We may even settle the marriage problem if we talk *honestly*. [Theodore *returns from telephoning to the sanitarium.*] Theodore, it's all right! John honestly believes in setting an example to society! Crazy to have his sisters go and do likewise!

Theodore

Splendid, John! I knew you'd see it — an ideal match.

Judge

[*overriding* John]

Right, Theodore, ideal. This scientific suitor will shower everything upon her John honors and admires: A host of servants — I mean sacrifices; carriages and motors — I mean character and morals; just what her brother advocates in Sunday-school — for others. An ideal marriage.

John

[*hands in pockets*]

You think you're awfully funny, don't you? Humph! I do more for the Church, for education, art, science than all the rest of the family

"And So They Were Married"

combined. Incidentally, I'm not divorced. . . . But this is a practical world, Theodore, I've got to protect my own.

Lucy
[*returning*]

Helen will be here in a minute.

John
[*suddenly getting an idea*]

Ah! I have it! I know how to keep them apart!

Theodore

Be careful, John — these two love each other.

Judge

Yes, young people still fall in love. Whether we make it hard or easy for them — they *will* do it. But, mark my words, unless we *reform marriage*, there is going to be a sympathetic *strike* against it — as there is already against having children. Instead of making it harder to get apart, we've got to make it easier to stay together. Otherwise the ancient bluff will soon be called!

Lucy

Sssh! Here she comes.

"And So They Were Married"

THEODORE

Please don't talk this way before her.

JUDGE

All right, I'm not divorced yet, . . . still in the conspiracy of silence.

[HELEN *appears at the door. A sudden silence.*

HELEN

[*kissing* THEODORE *and* JUDGE *affectionately*]

I'm *so* sorry to hear about dear Mary. [*To* JUDGE.] But why didn't Aunt Julia come? Is she ill, too? [*Slight panic in the family party.*

JUDGE

She's gone to Re-Re-Rio Janeiro — I mean to Santa Barbara — wants a complete change — The Rest Cure. [*To* THEODORE *apart.*] Lie number one.

[*Another silence.* LUCY *makes tea for* HELEN.

HELEN
[*taking the cup*]

Well, go on!

THEODORE

Go on with what?

"And So They Were Married"

Helen
[*stirring tea*]
Your discussion of marriage.

Lucy
How did you know?

Helen
Oh, it's in the air. Everybody's talking about it nowadays.
[*She sips tea, and the others look conscious.*

Theodore
My dear, marriage is woman's only true career.

Helen
[*raising her shield of flippancy*]
So Lucy tells me, Cousin Theodore. But a woman cannot pursue her career, she must be pursued by it; otherwise she is unwomanly.

Judge
Ahem. As we passed through the library a while ago, I think I saw your little sister being pursued by her career.

Helen
Yes, uncle, but Jean is a true woman. I'm only a New Woman.

"And So They Were Married"

Judge

All the same, you'll be an old woman some day — if you don't watch out.

Helen

Ah, yes, my life's a failure. I haven't trapped a man into a contract to support me.

Lucy

[*picks up knitting bag and does her best to look like "just an old-fashioned wife"*]

You ought to be ashamed! Making marriage so mercenary. Helen, dear, haven't you New Women any sentiment?

Helen

Enough sentiment not to make a mercenary marriage, Lucy, dear.

Judge

Ahem! And what kind of a marriage do you expect to make?

Helen

Not any, thank you, uncle.

Judge

What! You don't believe in holy matrimony?

"And So They Were Married"

Helen

Only as a last extremity, uncle, like unholy divorce.

Judge
[*jumps*]

What do *you* know about that?

Helen

I know all about it! [*Others jump.*] I have been reading up on the subject.
  [*All relax, relieved, but now gather about the young woman.*

Theodore
Come now, simply because many young people rush into marriage without thinking —

Lucy
Simply because these New Women —

John
Simply because one marriage in a thousand ends in divorce —

[*Together*]

"And So They Were Married"

Helen

Wait! . . . One in a thousand? Dear me, what an idealist you are, John! In America, one marriage in every eleven now ends in divorce. And yet you wonder why I hesitate.

John

One in eleven — rot! [*To* Judge.] All this muck-raking should be suppressed by the Government. "One in eleven!" Bah!

Helen
[*demurely*]

The Government's own statistics, John.
> [*They all turn to the* Judge *for denial, but he nods confirmation, with a complacent smile, murmuring:* "*Two souls with but a single thought.*"]

Lucy
[*sweetly knitting*]

Well, I may be old-fashioned, but it seems to *me* that nice girls shouldn't *think* of such things. . . . Their husbands will tell them all they ought to know about marriage — after they're married.

"And So They Were Married"

Helen

Ah, I see. Nice girls mustn't think until after they rush in, but they mustn't rush in until after they think. You married people make it all so simple for us.

Judge

Right! The way to cure all evil is for nice people to close their minds and mouths to it. It's "unpleasant" for a pure mind, and it "leaves a bad taste in the mouth." So there you are, my dear.

John

[coming in strong]

Oh, talk, talk, talk! I've had enough. See here, young lady, I offered to pay all your expenses abroad for a year. You didn't seem to appreciate it — well, the trustees of the institute are now to give Doctor Hamilton a year abroad. How do you like that?

[All turn and look at Helen.]

Helen

Splendid! Just what he needs! Doctor Metchnikoff told me in Paris that America always kills its big men with routine. When do we start? [*She tries to look very businesslike.*

JOHN
[*springing to his feet*]
"We!" Do you think *you* are going?

HELEN
Of course! I'm his assistant — quite indispensable to him . . . [*To all.*] Oh, well, if you don't believe me, ask him!

JOHN
[*pacing to and fro*]
What next! Paris! Alone, with a man! — Here's where I call a halt!

HELEN
But if my work calls me, I don't really see what you have to say about it, John.

JOHN
Better not defy me, Helen.   [*He scowls.*

HELEN
Better not bully me, John.   [*She smiles.*

"And So They Were Married"

John

I am your brother.

Helen

But not my owner! [*Then, instead of defiance, she turns with animated interest to the others.*] You know, all women used to be owned by men. Formerly they ruled us by physical force — now by financial force. . . . But at last they are to lose even *that* hold upon us — poor dears!

[*Pats* John's *shoulder playfully.*

John

[*amused, but serious*]

That's all right in theory, but this is a practical world. My pull got you into the institute; my pull can get you out. You give up this wild idea or give up your job!

Helen

[*delighted*]

What did I tell you? Financial force! They still try it, you see. [*To* John.] What if I refused to give up either, John?

"And So They Were Married"

JOHN
[*emphatic*]

Then as a trustee of the institute I ask for your resignation — right here and now! [*Turns away.*] I guess *that* will hold her at home a while.

HELEN

I simply *must* go to Paris now. I've nothing else to do!

JOHN
[*with a confident smile*]

You will, eh? Who'll pay your expenses this time?

HELEN
[*matter of fact*]

Doctor Hamilton.

LUCY

Helen! please! You oughtn't to say such things even in joke.

HELEN

He'll take me along as his private secretary, if I ask him.

  [*A pause. The others look at one another helplessly.*

"And So They Were Married"

Judge
John, she's got you. You might as well quit.

John
Nonsense. I have just begun. You'll see.

Theodore
If you're so independent, my dear, why don't you marry your scientist and be done with it?

Helen
[*resents the intrusion but hides her feelings*]
Can you keep a secret? [*They all seem to think they can and gather near.*] He has never asked me! [*The family seems annoyed.*

Lucy
[*with match-making ardor*]
No wonder, dear, he has never seen you except in that awful apron. But those stunning dinner gowns John bought you in Paris! My dear, in evening dress you are quite irresistible!

Judge
[*apart to* Theodore]
Irresistible? Pink parasols. What a system!

"And So They Were Married"

Helen

But you see, I don't *want* him to ask me. I've had all I could do to keep him from it.

> [*The family seems perplexed.*

John

She's got *some* sense left.

Lucy

But suppose he did ask you, dear?

Helen

Why, I'd simply refer the matter to John, of course. If John said, "Love him," I'd love him; if John said, "Don't love him," I'd turn it off like electric light.

> [*The family is becoming exasperated.*

Lucy

> [*insinuating*]

Oh, you can't deceive us. We know how much you admire him, Helen.

Helen

Oh, no you don't! [*The family is amazed.*] Not even he does. Did you ever hear how he

"And So They Were Married"

risked his life in battle down in Cuba? Why, he's a perfect hero of romance!

John
[*mutters*]

Never even saw a war — mollycoddle germ killer!

Helen

Not in the war with Spain — the war against yellow fever, John. . . . No drums to make him brave, no correspondents to make him famous — he merely rolled up his sleeve and let an innocent-looking mosquito bite him. Then took notes on his symptoms till he became delirious. . . . He happened to be among those who recovered. [*The family is impressed.*

Theodore

Old-fashioned maidens used to marry their heroes, Helen.

Helen
[*arising, briskly*]

But this new-fashioned hero gets only two thousand dollars a year, Theodore.

[*She turns to escape.*

"And So They Were Married"

John
[*nodding*]

I told you she had sense.

Theodore

Helen! You selfish, too? Why, Mary and I married on half that, didn't we, John?
[*He looks around. The family looks away.*

Helen
[*with unintended emphasis*]

Doctor Hamilton needs every cent of that enormous salary — books, travel, scientific conferences — all the advantages he simply must have if he's to keep at the top and do his best work for the world. The most selfish thing a girl can do is to marry a poor man.
[*With that she hurries up the steps.*

Theodore
[*following her*]

All the same, deep down under it all, she has a true woman's yearning for a home to care for and a mate to love. [*She is silently crying.*] Why, Helen, dear, what's the matter?

"And So They Were Married"

HELEN
[*hiding her emotion*]

Oh, why can't they let me *alone!* They make what ought to be the holiest and most beautiful thing in life the most horrible and dishonest. They make me hate marriage — hate it!

[*Unseen by* HELEN, *the* BUTLER *steps out.*

THEODORE
[*patting her shoulder*]

Just you wait till the right one comes along.

BUTLER
[*to* LUCY]

Doctor Hamilton has come, ma'am.

HELEN
[*with an old-fashioned gasp*]

Good heavens! [*And runs to the family.*

LUCY

Show Doctor Hamilton out.

[*The* BUTLER *goes.*

HELEN

A plot to entrap him! [*Running to and fro*

"And So They Were Married"

wildly.] But it's no use! I'm going . . . until he's gone!   [HELEN *runs into the garden.*

JUDGE
Fighting hard, poor child.

THEODORE
But what'll we do?

JUDGE
Don't worry — she can't stay away — the sweet thing!

JOHN
Now listen, we must all jolly him up — he'll be shy in these surroundings.

JUDGE
Going to surrender, John?

JOHN
What I am going to do requires finesse.

LUCY
[*in a flutter, seeing* HAMILTON *approach*]
Oh, dear! how does one talk to highbrows?

"And So They Were Married"

Judge

Talk to him about himself! Highbrows, lowbrows, all men love it.

> [Ernest Hamilton, *discoverer of the Hamilton antitoxin, is a fine-looking fellow of about thirty-five, without the spectacles or absent-mindedness somehow expected of scientific genius. He talks little but very rapidly and sees everything. It does not occur to him to be shy or embarrassed "in these surroundings" — not because he is habituated to so much luxury, on three thousand a year, nor because he despises it; he likes it; but he likes other things even more. That is why he works for two thousand a year, instead of working for fat, fashionable fees in private practice.*
>
> John *meets his distinguished guest at the door — effusively, yet with that smiling condescension which wealthy trustees sometimes show to "scientists, college professors, and that sort of thing."*

John

Ah, Doctor Hamilton! Delighted to see you on my little farm at last. Out here I'm just a plain, old-fashioned farmer.

"And So They Were Married"

[ERNEST *glances about at the magnificence and smiles imperceptibly. He makes no audible replies to the glad welcome, but bows urbanely, master of himself and the situation.*

LUCY

Doctor Hamilton! So good of you to come.

THEODORE

How are you, Ernest? Glad to see you.

LUCY

I don't think you've met our uncle, Judge Grey.

JUDGE

[*humorously adopting their manner*]
Charmed! I've heard so much about you!— from my niece.

LUCY

[*to* ERNEST'S *rescue, like a tactful hostess*]
A cup of tea, Doctor Hamilton?

ERNEST

[*unperturbed by the reference to* HELEN]
Thanks.

"AND SO THEY WERE MARRIED"

JOHN

[*while* LUCY *makes tea. Trustee manner*]

I have often desired to express my admiration of your heroism in the war against yellow fever in er — ah — *Cuba*, when you let an innocent-looking mosquito bite you ——

LUCY

[*nodding and poising sugar-tongs*]

And then took notes on your symptoms till you became delirious!

ERNEST

No sugar, thanks.

[*He looks from one to another with considerable interest.*

JUDGE

No drums to make you famous, no war correspondents to make you brave — I mean the other way round.

ERNEST

[*to* LUCY *poising cream pitcher*]

No cream, please.

JOHN

Senator Root says this one triumph alone

saves *twenty million dollars a year* to the business interests of the United States! I call that true patriotism.

ERNEST
[*with a nod of assent to* LUCY]

Lemon.

THEODORE
[*with sincerity*]

General Wood says it saves more *human lives* a year than were lost in the whole Spanish War! I call it service.

JUDGE

Colonel Goethals says the Panama Canal could not have been built if it hadn't been for you self-sacrificing scientists. Not only that, but you have abolished forever from the United States a scourge which for more than a century had through periodic outbreaks spread terror, devastation, and death. [*A pause.*

ERNEST
[*bored, but trying to hide it*]

The ones who deserve your praise are the four who died to prove that theory.... [*He smiles.*] Of course, you all know their names.... [*He

"And So They Were Married"

looks at JOHN, *who looks at* JUDGE, *who looks at* LUCY, *who looks at* THEODORE. *He takes up his cup.*] Delicious tea.

THEODORE

Ah, but they didn't do it for fame, for money — that's the beauty of the sacrifice.

ERNEST
[*with a smile*]

Quite so. . . . That's what Congress told us when we suggested a pension for the widow of the first victim.

ALL

What! Did Congress refuse the pension?

ERNEST
[*finishes his tea*]

They finally voted the sum of seventeen dollars a month for the widow and no less than two dollars a month extra for each of his children. . . .

LUCY

Is that all?

"And So They Were Married"

Ernest

No. . . . We pestered Congress to death until, a few years ago, they replaced the pension with an annuity of one hundred and twenty-five dollars a month — though some of them said it was a very bad precedent to establish. [*Returns cup to* Lucy.] No more, thanks, delicious.

[*And turns to admire the wide-sweeping view of the farm, hands in pockets.*

John
[*after a pause*]

Well, I think our scientists might well be called philanthropists.

Ernest

Hardly! You see, every one *knows* the names of philanthropists. . . . Better let it go at "scientists."

Judge

He's right. Philanthropists don't give their lives, they give their names—have 'em carved in stone over their institutes and libraries.

[John *approaches and joins his guest.*

Ernest

Charming little farm you have here.

"And So They Were Married"

John

Doctor Hamilton, America kills its big men with routine. You are too valuable to the nation to lose — the trustees think you need a year abroad.

Ernest

That's strange, I came out here to suggest that very thing. . . . Somebody has been saying kind things about me in Paris. Just had a letter from the great Metchnikoff — wants me to come over and work in the Pasteur! Chance of a lifetime! . . . You didn't have to jolly me up to consent to that!

John

[*pacing terrace with his guest, arm in arm*]
By the by, my sister is rather keen on science.

Ernest

Best assistant I ever had. You can pile an awful lot of routine on a woman. The female of the species is more faithful than the male. . . . She's over there already. We can get right to work.

John

She'll be back before you start.

"And So They Were Married"

Ernest
[*stops short*]
I didn't know that. . . . Well, what is it?
[JOHN *hesitates, turns to the family, all watching with breathless interest.*

Theodore
Don't you see, old chap, under the circumstances it would hardly do for her to go back to Paris with you.

Ernest
Why not?

Lucy
You're a man.

Ernest
[*smiling*]
You mean I'm dangerous?

Lucy
But she's a woman.

Judge
They mean *she's* dangerous.

"And So They Were Married"

John

My dear fellow, we are going to ask you quite frankly to decline to take her.

Ernest

[*looks about at the circle of anxious faces. He won't let them read him*]

So that's it, eh? . . . But it's the chance of a lifetime for her, too. She needs it more than I do. She's had so little chance to do original work.

John

But she's a woman.

Ernest

Just what has that to do with it?

John

Everything. We have the highest respect for you, Doctor Hamilton, but also . . . one must respect the opinions of the world, you know.

Ernest

[*thinks it over*]

That's right. One must. I forgot to think of that. . . . It's curious, but when working with women of ability one learns to respect them so much that one quite loses the habit of insulting them. Too bad how new conditions spoil fine old customs. . . . Suppose you let her go and let me stay. I can find plenty to do here, I fancy.

John

I fear it would offend our generous benefactor, Mr. Baker. He has set his heart on your going abroad, meeting other big men, getting new ideas for our great humanitarian work. [*The family exchange glances while* John *lies on.*] Besides, my sister would only go to accommodate you. She particularly desires to stay here this winter. That's why she is returning so soon, you see.

Ernest
[*believes it*]

Oh, I see. . . . I'm sure I have no desire to *drag* her over with me. . . . [*Smiles at himself.*] I rather thought the opportunity to continue our experiments together . . . but that's all right.

John

Then it's all settled — you agree to go alone?

"And So They Were Married"

ERNEST
[*a slight pause*]
Yes, alone. It's quite settled.

JOHN
How soon could you start?

ERNEST
[*absently*]
How soon? Why, just as soon as I get some one to run my department.

JOHN
Could my sister run it?

ERNEST
[*smiles*]
Could she run it? It can't run without her! She's as systematic as [*to* LUCY] — as a good housekeeper.

JOHN
[*with a satisfied look at the others*]
Then *that's* all fixed! She'll stay when I tell her that you want her to. Could you arrange to start at once?

"And So They Were Married"

Ernest
[hesitates]
By leaving here to-night, I could.

John
[with a triumphant look at the family]
Then I'll telephone for your passage — I have a pull with all the steamship lines. *[Going.]* Of course I hate to cut short your week-end, but I don't want to spoil any scientific careers.

> [John *hurries in to telephone.* Ernest *starts too, as if to stop him but restrains the impulse. He stands alone by the door gazing out over the landscape while* Lucy, Theodore, *and the* Judge *discuss him in low tones by the tea-table.*

Lucy
Can't you see, you stupid men! He's crazy about her — but thinks there's no hope.

Theodore
When she finds he's leaving for a year . . . she'll change her mind about marriage!

> [Ernest *comes back to earth and to the house-party.*

"And So They Were Married"

Judge
[*to* Ernest, *joining them*]

Ahem! We were just discussing the marriage danger — I mean the marriage problem.

Ernest
[*with a smile*]

Go right on — don't mind me.

Theodore
[*old-friend manner*]

See here! When are *you* ever going to marry?

Ernest
[*modern bachelor's laugh*]

When am I ever going to get more than two thousand a year?

Theodore

Bah! what has money got to do with it! Just you wait till the right one comes along.

> [Helen *comes along, stealing up the steps from the garden on tiptoe with the grave, absorbed look of a hunter stalking game. She catches sight of the man she wants and stops short, as motionless as if frozen. But not so! Her lovely hands were poised;*

"And So They Were Married"

one of them now goes to her bosom and presses there. There is nothing icy about this New Woman now.

Ernest

[*as unconscious of danger as a mountain-lion on an inaccessible height, smiles easily at his sentimental old friend* Theodore]

How do you know "the right one" hasn't come already?

[Theodore *catches sight of* Helen. *She shakes her head in silent pleading, taps a finger on her lips, and in a panic flees noiselessly across toward the door.*

Theodore

[*suppressing a laugh*]

Then don't let her go by!

[Helen *stops at the door and makes a face at* Theodore.

Ernest

[*affecting indifference*]

Oh, I couldn't stop her, even if I wanted to.

Theodore

[*turning to wink at* Helen]

How do you know? Did you ever ask her?

"And So They Were Married"

Ernest

To marry me? Oh, no! She hasn't any money.

Theodore

[Helen *is dumfounded*]

Money! You wouldn't marry for money!

[Helen *draws near to hear the answer.*

Ernest

You don't suppose I'd marry a woman who hadn't any? Most selfish thing a poor man can do.   [Helen *is interested.*

Theodore

Oh, fiddlesticks! You modern young people —

Ernest

[*interrupts*]

Make her a sort of superior servant in an inferior home — not that girl! [Helen *is pleased.*

Theodore

Feministic nonsense! The old-fashioned womanly woman ——

"And So They Were Married"

Ernest

Sentimental twaddle! What makes it more "womanly" to do menial work *for* men than intellectual work with them?

    [Helen *delighted, applauds noiselessly.*

Theodore

All the same, I'll bet you wouldn't let a little thing like that stand in your way if you really cared for a woman enough to marry her.

Ernest

[benign and secure]

But, as it happens, I don't. Nothing could induce me to marry.

    [Helen *raises her chin, her eyes glitter dangerously.*

Theodore

So you are going to run away to Europe like a coward?

Ernest

[smiles patronizingly]

Theodore, you are such an incorrigible idealist! I have nothing to be afraid of — I simply do not care to *marry!*

"And So They Were Married"

Helen
That's just what *I* said!
> [*All turn and behold* Helen.

Ernest
My heavens! [*He steps back like a coward.*

Helen
But I agree with you perfectly. [*She holds out her hand to him.*] I was *so* afraid you believed in marriage.   [*He rushes to her eagerly.*

Judge
[*as the lovers shake hands*]
You wronged him. Apologize.

Ernest
Why — why — all this time, I thought *you* had the usual attitude.

Judge
Wronged *her*. Both apologize.

Helen
Why didn't you ever tell me you had such enlightened views?

"And So They Were Married"

Ernest

Why didn't you ever tell me?

Judge

Each understands the other now. Everything lovely!

Helen

Think of the discussions we might have had!

Judge

Not too late yet. Julia and I had discussions for a quarter of a century.

Helen

Don't think I had any hand in this. [*Laughs.*] I was going to warn you, but now — it is unnecessary now.

Ernest

Warn me? What do you mean?

Helen

Can't you see? It was all a plot! [Lucy *draws near noiselessly.*] A plot to entrap you in marriage! They had about given me up as a bad

"AND SO THEY WERE MARRIED"

job. *You* were my last hope. They were going to throw me at your head. [*Louder but without turning.*] Weren't you, Lucy dear?

LUCY
[*caught listening, turns abruptly to the others*]
These New Women are utterly shameless.

HELEN
[*to* ERNEST]

These old-fashioned women are utterly shameless. After a decent interval, they will all with one accord make excuses to leave us here alone, so that I can — [*she comes nearer*] ensnare you! [ERNEST *laughs nervously.*] Lucy is going to say — [*imitates* LUCY's *sweet tones*]: "If you'll excuse me, I always take forty winks before dressing." Dressing is the hardest work Lucy has to do. Cousin Theodore will find that he *must* write to his wife, and Uncle Everett will feel a yearning for the billiard room. [ERNEST *is nodding and chuckling.*] They're hanging on longer than usual to-day, and I simply must have a talk with you.

ERNEST
Our shop-talk would scandalize 'em!

"And So They Were Married"

Helen

Wait, I'll get rid of them!

[*She sits and begins to make tea.*

Ernest

I've had my tea, thanks.

Helen

Stupid! Sit down. [*Indicates a chair close to hers. He takes it cautiously.*] We'll have a little fun with them in a minute.

[*She is busy now making tea.*

Theodore

[*to* Lucy *and the* Judge *apart*]

You may be right, Uncle Everett, but upon my word it is the strangest courtship I ever witnessed.

Lucy

They ought to be spanked.

Judge

Don't worry, old Mother Nature will attend to that.

Lucy

Well, I may be old-fashioned, but ——

"And So They Were Married"

Judge
[interrupting]

But this is merely a new fashion, my dear Lucy. Nature her ancient custom holds, let science say what it will.

Helen
[handing cup to Ernest *with a glance at the others]*

Now, then, be attentive to me. *[He leans toward her rather shyly, abashed by her nearness. She makes eyes at him reproachfully.]* Oh, can't you be more attentive than *that?* *[She acts like a coquette and he looks into her beautiful eyes and while he is doing so she says with a fascinating drawl]* Now tell me a-all about anterior poliomyelitis!

Ernest
[suddenly taken aback, he laughs]

Nothing doing since you left.

[And bends close to explain.

Lucy
If you'll excuse me, Doctor Hamilton, I

"And So They Were Married"

always take forty winks before dressing. We dine at eight.

[*Going, she signals to the others.* ERNEST *and* HELEN *exchange smiles.*

THEODORE
[*laughing, to* LUCY]

Ss't! Don't tell John what's going on! Keep him busy telephoning. [LUCY *nods excitedly and almost runs to obey the Church.*] Helen, if you and Ernest will excuse me, I really must write to Mary.

[*Their shoulders are close together and they seem too absorbed to reply.* THEODORE *smiles down upon them and signals the* JUDGE *to come along. The* JUDGE, *however, shakes his head but waves* THEODORE *into the house. Uncle Everett looks at the lovers with quizzical interest. He draws near and eavesdrops shamelessly.*

HELEN

You oughtn't to have dropped the polio experiments.

ERNEST

You oughtn't to have dropped me — right in the *midst* of the experiments. Those agar

"And So They Were Married"

plates you were incubating dried up and spoiled. You played the very devil with my data.

Judge

God bless my soul! what are we coming to?

Helen
[*without turning*]

It's perfectly proper for your little ears, uncle, only you can't understand a word of it. Won't *any* one play billiards with you?

Judge

But I'm fascinated. It's so idyllic. Makes me feel young again.

Helen
[*to* Ernest]

Oh, you have plenty of men assistants who can estimate antitoxin units.

Ernest

Men assistants lose interest. They are all so confoundedly ambitious to do original work. Why is it women can stand day after day of monotonous detail better than men?

"And So They Were Married"

Helen

Because men always made them tend the home!

Judge

Ah, nothing like a good old-fashioned love scene — in the scientific spirit.

Helen

Uncle, dear! *Can't* you see that he is paying me wonderful compliments? Haven't you any tact? Go and play Canfield in the library.

Judge
[*lighting cigar*]

Very well, I'll leave you to your own devices — and may God, *your* God, have mercy on your scientific souls.

Helen
[*with sudden animation and camaraderie, thinking they are alone*]

Now I must tell you what Doctor Metchnikoff said about you and your future!

Judge

Sst! [Helen *and* Ernest *turn*.] My children

"And So They Were Married"

— [*Pause — raises his hand.*] Don't forget the scientific spirit!

[*The* Judge *saunters off into the garden, smoking.*]

Ernest
How did you ever meet Metchnikoff?

Helen
[*chaffing*]

I had worked under Hamilton! They *all* wanted to meet me.

Ernest
[*with an unmistakable look*]

U'm . . . was that why? [*Fleeing danger.*] Didn't you let them know your part in that discovery? Why, if it hadn't been for you, I should never have stumbled upon the thing at all.

Helen
Oh, I know my place too well for that! Talk about *artistic* temperament, you scientists are worse than prima donnas.

Ernest
[*takes printers' proofs out of pocket, hands them to her in silence*]

Some proofs of a monograph I was correcting

"And So They Were Married"

on the train. Mind hammering those loose sentences of mine into decent English? You can write — I can't.

HELEN
[*reading innocently*]

"Recent Experiments in Anterior Poliomyelitis by Ernest Hamilton, M.D., Ph.D., and Helen" — what! why, you've put *my* name with yours! [*Much excited and delighted.*

ERNEST

Well, if you object — like a prima donna ——
[*Takes out pencil to mark on proof.*

HELEN
[*snatching proofs away*]

Object? Why, this makes my reputation in the scientific world.

ERNEST

Well, didn't you make mine?

HELEN
[*still glowing with pride, but touched by his unexpected generosity*]

You can't imagine what this means to me. It's so hard for a woman to get any recognition.

"And So They Were Married"

Most men have but one use for us. If we get interested in anything but *them* it is "unwomanly" — they call it "a fad." But they've *got* to take me seriously now. My name with Ernest Hamilton's!

> [*Points to her name and swaggers back and forth.*

Ernest
[*bantering*]

But then, you see, you are a very exceptional woman. Why, you have a mind like a man.

Helen

Like a man? [*Coming close to him, tempting him.*] If you had a mind like a woman you would know better than to say that to me!

> [*Re-enter* Judge *from garden. He smiles and glances at them. The lovers keep quiet as he crosses to the door. Then they look at each other and smile.* Judge *has gone into the house. It is nearly dark. The moon is rising.*

Ernest
[*raises eyebrows*]

They all take for granted that I want to make love to you.   [*Smiles but avoids her eyes.*

"And So They Were Married"

HELEN

[*avoids his*]

Well, you took for granted that I wanted you to! . . . You are about the most conceited man I ever knew.

ERNEST

How can I help it when you admire me so?

HELEN

I? Admire you?

ERNEST

You're always telling me what great things I'm going to do — stimulating me, pushing me along. Why, after you left, everything went slump. Tell me, why did you leave? Was I rude to you? Did I hurt your feelings?

HELEN

Not in the least. It was entirely out of respect for *your* feelings.

ERNEST

My feelings? [*Laughing.*] Oh, I see. You got it into your head that *I* wanted to marry *you!*

"And So They Were Married"

Helen

Men sometimes do.

Ernest
[looks away]

I suppose they do.

Helen

It's been known to happen.

Ernest

Talk about conceit! Well, you needn't be afraid! I'll never ask you to marry *me*.

Helen
[turns and looks at him a moment]

You can't imagine what a weight this takes off my mind.　　*[She looks away and sighs.*

Ernest
[enthusiastically]

Yes! I feel as if a veil between us had been lifted.

[He looks away and sighs too. Some one begins- "Tristan and Isolde" on the piano within. The moon is up.

"And So They Were Married"

Helen
[*after a pause*]
Suppose we talk about — our work.

Ernest
Yes! Our work. Let's drop the other subject. Look at the moon!
[*Music and the moonlight flooding them.*

Helen
Seriously, you promise never to *mention* the subject again? [*She keeps her eyes averted.*

Ernest
I promise. [*He keeps his eyes averted.*

Helen
[*turning to him with a sudden change to girlish enthusiasm*]
Then I'll go to Paris with you!

Ernest
[*recoils*]
What's that?

Helen
Why, Doctor Metchnikoff — he promised me he would invite you.

"And So They Were Married"

ERNEST

Yes, but —

HELEN

Don't miss the chance of a lifetime!

ERNEST

No, but you — *you* can't come!

HELEN
[*simply*]

If you need me I can, and you just said ——

ERNEST

But you mustn't come to Paris with me!

HELEN

Don't you want me with you?

ERNEST

You are to stay at home and run the department for me.

HELEN
[*stepping back*]

Don't you want me with you?

"And So They Were Married"

Ernest

[*stepping forward, with his heart in voice*]

Do I *want* you! [*Stops.*] But I am a man — you are a woman.

Helen

What of it? Are you one of those small men who care what people say? No! That's not your reason! [*She sees that it is not.*] What is it? You must tell me.

Ernest

[*hesitates*]

It's only for your sake.

Helen

[*with feeling*]

Think of all I've done for *your* sake. You wouldn't be going yourself but for me! I was the one to see you needed it, I proposed it to Metchnikoff — I urged him — *made* him ask you — for *your sake!* And now am I to be left at home like a child because you don't care to be embarrassed with me?

Ernest

Oh, please! This is so unfair. But I simply can't take you now.

"And So They Were Married"

Helen
[*with growing scorn*]

Oh! You are all alike. You pile work upon me until I nearly drop, you play upon my interest, my sympathy — you get all you can out of me — my youth, my strength, my best! And then, just as I, too, have a chance to arrive in my profession, you, of all men, throw me over! I hate men. I hate you!

Ernest

And I love you!

[*They stare at each other in silence, the moonlight flooding* Helen's *face, the music coming clear.*

Helen
[*in an awed whisper, stepping back slowly*]

I've done it! I've done it! I *knew* I'd do it!

Ernest

No. I did it. Forgive me. I had to do it.

Helen

Oh, and this spoils everything!

"And So They Were Married"

Ernest
[*comes closer*]

No! It glorifies everything! [*He breaks loose.*] I have loved you from the first day you came and looked up at me for orders. I didn't want you there; I didn't want any woman there. I tried to tire you out with overwork but couldn't. I tried to drive you out by rudeness, but you stayed. And that made me love you more. Oh, I love you! I love you! I love you!

Helen
Don't; oh, don't love me!

Ernest
[*still closer*]

Why, I never knew there could be women like you. I thought women were merely something to be wanted and worshipped, petted and patronized. But now — why, I love everything about you: your wonderful, brave eyes that face the naked facts of life and are not ashamed; those beautiful hands that toiled so long, so well, so close to mine and not afraid, not afraid!

Helen
You mustn't! I *am* afraid now! I made you

"And So They Were Married"

say it. [*Smiling and crying.*] I have always wanted to make you say it. I have always sworn you shouldn't.

Ernest
[*pained*]

Because you cannot care enough?

Helen

Enough? . . . Too much.

Ernest
[*overwhelmed*]

You — love — me!

[*He takes her in his arms, a silent embrace with only the bland blasé moon looking on.*]

Helen

It is because I love you that I didn't want you to say it — only I did. It is because I love you that I went abroad — to stay, only I couldn't! I couldn't stay away! [*She holds his face in her hands.*] Oh, do you know how I love you? No! . . . you're only a *man*!

Ernest
[*kissing her rapturously*]

Every day there in the laboratory, when you

"And So They Were Married".

in your apron — that dear apron which I stole from your locker when you left me — when you asked for orders — did you know that I wanted to say: "Love me"! Every day when you took up your work, did you never guess that I wanted to take you up in my arms?

Helen
[*smiling up into his face*]
Why didn't you?

Ernest
Thank God I didn't! For while we worked there together I came to know you as few men ever know the women they desire. Woman can be more than sex, as man is more than sex. And all this makes man and woman not less but more *overwhelmingly* desirable and necessary to each other, and makes both things last — not for a few years, but forever!

[*Sound of voices approaching from the garden. The lovers separate. It is* Jean *and* Rex, Rex *laughing,* Jean *dodging until caught and kissed.*]

Jean
No, no — it's time to dress. . . . Be good, Rex — don't!

"And So They Were Married"

[*Without seeing* Helen *and* Ernest, *they disappear into the house.* Helen *is suddenly changed, as if awakened from a spell of enchantment.*

Helen

What have we done! This is all moonlight and madness. To-morrow comes the clear light of day.

Ernest

Ah, but we'll love each other to-morrow!

Helen

But we cannot marry — then or any other to-morrow.

Ernest

Can't? What nonsense!

Helen

[*shaking her head and restraining him*]
I have slaved for you all these months — not because I wanted to win you from your work but to help you in it. And now — after all — shall I destroy you? No! No!

"And So They Were Married"

Ernest

I *love* you — you love *me* — nothing else matters.

Helen

Everything else matters. I'm not a little débutante to be persuaded that I am needed because I am wanted! I haven't *played* with you; I have *worked* with you, and I *know!* Think of Theodore! Think of Lucy! And now poor little Jean. Marry you? Never!

Ernest

You mean your career?

Helen

[*with supreme scorn*]

My career? No! yours — always yours!

Ernest

[*with the same scorn and a snap of the fingers*]

Then *that* for my career. I'll go back into private practice and make a million.

Helen

That's just what I said you'd do. Just what you must not do! Your work is needed by the world.

"And So They Were Married"

Ernest
[*wooing*]

You are my world and I need you. . . . But there is no love without marriage, no marriage without money. . . . We can take it or leave it. Can we leave it? No! I can't — you can't! Come! [*She steps back slowly.*] Why should we sacrifice the best! Come!

Helen

So *this* is what marriage means! Then I *cannot* marry you, Ernest!

Ernest

You cannot do without me, Helen! [*Holds out his arms.*] Come! You have been in my arms once. You and I can never forget that now. We can never go back now. It's all — or nothing now. Come! [*She is struggling against her passion. He stands still, with arms held out.*] I shall not woo you against your will, but you are coming to me! Because, by all the powers of earth and heaven, you are mine and I am yours! Come!

[*Like a homing pigeon she darts into his arms with a gasp of joy. A rapturous embrace in*

"And So They Were Married"

silence with the moonlight streaming down upon them. The music has stopped.

JOHN, *dressed for dinner, strolls out upon the terrace. He stops abruptly upon discovering them. The lovers are too absorbed to be aware of his presence.*

Act II

Act II

It is the next morning, Sunday.

It appears that at John's *country place they have breakfast at small tables out upon the broad, shaded terrace overlooking the glorious view of his little farm.*

Ernest *and* Theodore, *the scientist and the clergyman, are breakfasting together. The others are either breakfasting in their rooms or are not yet down, it being Sunday.*

The man of God is enjoying his material blessings heartily. Also he seems to be enjoying his view of the man of science, who eats little and says less.

Theodore

[*with coffee-cup poised*]

WHAT'S the matter with your appetite this morning, Ernest? [Ernest, *gazing up at one of the second-story windows, does not hear. The door opens. He starts. Then, seeing it's only a servant with food, he*

"And So They Were Married"

sighs.] Expecting something? The codfish balls? Well, here they are. [ERNEST *refuses the proffered codfish balls, scowls, brings out cigar case, lights cigar, looks at watch, and fidgets.*] Oh, I know — you're crazy to go with me — to church! [ERNEST *doesn't hear. Creates a cloud of smoke.*] Their regular rector is ill. So I agreed to take the service this morning. . . . Always the way when off for a rest . . . isn't it? [*No answer.* THEODORE *gets up, walks around the table, and shouts in* ERNEST'S *face.*] Isn't it?

ERNEST
[*startled*]

I beg your pardon?

THEODORE
[*laughs,* ERNEST *wondering what's the joke*]

Oh, you're hopeless! [*Going.*] I can't stand people who talk so much at breakfast.

ERNEST
[*suddenly wakes up*]

Wait a minute. Sit down. Have a cigar. Let's talk about God. [THEODORE *stops smiling.*] But I mean it. I'd like to have a religion myself.

"And So They Were Married"

Theodore

I had an idea you took no stock in religion.

[Takes the cigar. Ernest holds a match for him.

Ernest
[enthusiastically]

Just what I thought, until . . . well, I've made a discovery, a great discovery!

Theodore

A scientific discovery?

Ernest
[with a wave of the hand]

It makes all science look like a . . . mere machine.

Theodore

Well, if you feel so strongly about it . . . better come to church after all!

Ernest

I'm not talking about the Church — I'm talking about *religion*.

"And So They Were Married"

THEODORE

You're not talking about religion; you're talking about — love.

ERNEST

[*quietly*]

Certainly; the same thing, isn't it? I'm talking about the divine fire that glorifies life and perpetuates it — the one eternal thing we mortals share with God. . . . If *that* isn't religious, what is? [THEODORE *smiles indulgently.*] Tell me, Theodore — you know I wasn't allowed to go to church when young, and since then I've always worked on the holy Sabbath day, like yourself — does the Church still let innocent human beings think there's something inherently wrong about sex? [THEODORE *drops his eyes.* ERNEST *disgusted with him.*] I see! Good people should drop their eyes even at the mention of the word.

THEODORE

Sex is a necessary evil, I admit, but ——

ERNEST

[*laughs*]

Evil! The God-given impulse which accounts for you sitting there, for me sitting here? The

"And So They Were Married"

splendid instinct which writes our poetry, builds our civilizations, founds our churches — the very heart and soul of life is evil. Really, Theodore, I don't know much about religion, but that strikes me as blasphemy against the Creator.

Theodore

Very scientific, my boy, very modern; but the Church believed in marriage before Science was born.

Ernest

As a compromise with evil?

Theodore

As a sacrament of religion — and so do you!

Ernest

Good! Then why practise and preach marriage as a sacrament of property? "Who giveth this woman to be married to this man —" Women are still goods and chattels to be given or sold, are they?

Theodore

Oh, nonsense!

"And So They Were Married"

ERNEST

Then why keep on making them promise to "serve and obey"? Why marry them with a ring — the link of the ancient chain? [*He smiles.*] In the days of physical force it was made of iron — now of gold. But it's still a chain, isn't it?

THEODORE

Symbols, my dear fellow, not to be taken in a literal sense — time-honored and beautiful symbols.

ERNEST

But why insult a woman you respect — even symbolically?

THEODORE
[*with a laugh*]

Oh, you scientists!

ERNEST
[*joining in the laugh*]

We try to find the truth — and you try to hide it, eh? Well, there's one thing we have in common, anyway — one faith I'll never doubt again; I believe in Heaven now. I always shall.

"And So They Were Married"

Theodore
Do you mind telling me why, my boy?

Ernest
Not in the least. I've been there. [JOHN *comes out to breakfast. He is scowling.*] Good morning; could you spare me five minutes?

John
[*ringing bell*]

Haven't had breakfast yet.

Ernest
After breakfast?

John
I've an appointment with young Baker.

Ernest
[*smiles*]

I'll wait my turn.

John
Going to be pretty busy to-day — you, too, I suppose, if you're sailing to-morrow.

"And So They Were Married"

ERNEST

I can postpone sailing. This is more important.

JOHN

I should hate to see *anything* interfere with your career.

[LUCY *also arrives for breakfast. She "always pours her husband's coffee."*

ERNEST

I appreciate your interest, but I'll look out for my "career." [*To* LUCY.] Could you tell me when your sister will be down?

JOHN
[*overriding* LUCY]

My sister is ill and won't be down at all . . . until *after* you *leave*.

[LUCY *pretends not to hear.* THEODORE *walks away.*

ERNEST
[*aroused, but calm*]

I don't believe you quite understand. It is a matter of indifference to me whether we have a talk or not. Entirely out of courtesy to you that I suggest it.

"And So They Were Married"

John
Don't inconvenience yourself on my account.

Ernest
[*shrugs shoulders and turns to* Theodore]
Wait, I think I'll sit in church till train time.

Theodore
[*smoothing it over*]
Come along. I'm going to preach about marriage! [Theodore *starts off.*

Ernest
[*going, turns to* Lucy]
Thanks for your kindness. Will you ask the valet to pack my things, please? I'll call for them on the way to the station. [*To* John.] Do you understand? I have no favors to ask of you. You don't own your sister — she owns herself. [*The scientist goes to church.*

John
[*with a loud laugh, turns to* Lucy]
Rather impertinent for a two-thousand-dollar man, I think. [*Resumes breakfast, picks up newspaper.* Lucy *says nothing, attending to his*

"And So They Were Married"

wants solicitously.] Bah! what does this highbrow know about the power men of my sort can use ... when we have to? [LUCY *cringes dutifully in silence.* JOHN, *paper in one hand, brusquely passes cup to* LUCY *with other.*] Helen got her own way about college, about work, about living in her own apartment — but if she thinks she can put *this* across! Humph! These modern women must learn their place. [LUCY, *smiling timidly, returns cup.* JOHN *takes it without thanks, busied in newspapers. A look of resentment creeps over* LUCY'S *pretty face, now that he can't see her.*] Ah! I've got something up my sleeve for that young woman. [LUCY *says nothing, looks of contempt while he reads.*] Well, why don't you say something?

LUCY

[*startled*]

I thought you didn't like me to talk at breakfast, dear.

JOHN

Think I like you to sit there like a mummy? [*No reply.*] Haven't you *anything* to say? [*Apparently not.*] You never have any more, nothing interesting. ... Does it ever occur to you that I'd like to be diverted? ... No!

"And So They Were Married"

Lucy

Yes. . . . Would you mind very much if . . . if I left you, John?

John

Left me? When — where — how long?

Lucy

[*gathering courage*]

Now — any place — entirely.

John

[*bursts out laughing*]

What suddenly put *this* notion in your head?

Lucy

I'm sorry — John, but I've had it — oh, for years. I never dared ask you till now.

John

[*still glancing over paper*]

Like to leave me, would you? . . . You have no grounds for divorce, my dear.

Lucy

But *you* will have — after I leave you.

"And So They Were Married"

JOHN

[*yawns*]

You have no lover to leave with.

LUCY

[*daintily*]

But couldn't I just desert you — without anything horrid?

JOHN

[*reads*]

No money to desert with.

LUCY

[*springs up — at bay*]

You won't let me escape decently when I tell you I don't want to stay? When I tell you I can't stand being under your roof any longer? When I tell you I'm sick of this life?

JOHN

[*gets up calmly*]

But, you see, I can stand it. I want you to stay. I'm not sick of it. You belong to me.

LUCY

[*shrinking away as he approaches*]

Don't touch me! Every time you come near me I have to nerve myself to stand it.

"AND SO THEY WERE MARRIED"

JOHN

What's got into you? Don't I give you everything money can buy? My God, if I only gave you something to worry about; if I ran after other women like old man Baker ——

LUCY

If you only would! — Then you'd let *me* alone. To me you are repulsive.

JOHN
[*taking hold of her*]

Lucy! You are my wife.

LUCY
[*looking him straight in the eye*]

But you don't respect me, and I — I hate you — oh, how I hate you!

JOHN
[*holds her fast*]

I am your husband, your lawful husband.

LUCY
[*stops struggling*]

Yes, this is lawful — but, oh, what laws you men have made for women!

[*The* JUDGE *comes out, carrying a telegram.*

"And So They Were Married"

JUDGE

Rather early in the day for conjugal embraces, if you should ask me. [JOHN *and* LUCY *separate.*] Makes me quite sentimental and homesick.

[JUDGE *raises telegram and kisses it.*

LUCY

[*calming herself*]

From Aunt Julia again? Do you get telegrams every day from Reno?

JUDGE

No, but she caught cold. Went to the theatre last night and caught a cold. So she wired me — naturally; got the habit of telling me her troubles, can't break it, even in Reno.

JOHN

I thought she hated the theatre!

JUDGE

So she does, but I'm fond of it; she went for my sake. She's got the habit of sacrificing herself for me. Just as hard to break good habits as bad.

JOHN

True women enjoy sacrificing themselves.

"And So They Were Married"

Judge

Yes, that's what we tell them. Well, we ought to know. We make 'em do it. [*Brings out a fountain pen and sits abruptly.*] That's what I'll tell her. I can hear her laugh. You know her laugh.

Lucy

[*rings for a servant*]

A telegraph blank?

Judge

[*with a humorous expression he brings a whole pad of telegraph blanks out of another pocket*]

Carry them with me nowadays. [*Begins to write.*] Wish I hadn't sold my Western Union, John.

John

I don't believe you want that divorce very much.

Judge

It doesn't matter what *I* want — what she wants is the point. You must give the woman you marry tutti-frutti, divorces — everything.

... Why, I've got the habit myself, and God knows I don't enjoy sacrifice — I'm a man! The superior sex!

JOHN

I don't believe you appreciate that wife of yours.

JUDGE

[*between the words he's writing*]

Don't I? It isn't every wife that'd travel away out to Reno — you know how she hates travelling — and go to a theatre — and catch a cold —, and get a divorce — all for the sake of an uncongenial husband. [*Suddenly getting an idea, strikes table.*] I know what gave her a cold. She raised all the windows in her bedroom — for *my* sake! — I always kept them down for *her* sake. I'll have to scold her. [*Bends to his writing again.*] Poor little thing! She doesn't know how to take care of herself without me. I doubt if she ever will.

[*Looks over telegram. A* SERVANT *comes, takes telegram, and goes.*

JOHN

Uncle Everett, I want your advice.

"And So They Were Married"

Judge

John! do *you* want a divorce?

John

No, we are not that sort, are we, Lucy? [*No answer.*] *Are* we, dear?

Lucy

[*after a pause*]

No, we are not that sort!

John

We believe in the sanctity of the home, the holiness of marriage.

Lucy

Yes, we believe in — "the holiness of marriage!"

[*Turns away, covering her face with her hands and shuddering.*

John

Lucy, tell Helen and Jean to come here. [Lucy *goes.*] Well, young Baker spoke to me about Jean last night. I told him I'd think it over and give him my decision this morning.

"And So They Were Married"

Judge

That's right. Mustn't seem too anxious, John. When the properly qualified male offers one of our dependent females a chance at woman's only true career, of course it's up to us to look disappointed.

John

But I didn't bring up the little matter you spoke of.

Judge

About that chorus girl? . . . Afraid of scaring him off?

John

Not at all, but — well, it's all over and it's all fixed. No scandal, no blackmail.

Judge

Hum! By the way, got anything on Hamilton?

John

I don't believe in saints myself.

"And So They Were Married"

Judge

I see. . . . Good thing, for Jean Rex isn't a saint. I suppose you'd break off the match.

> [Rex, *in riding clothes, comes out.* John *salutes him warmly. The* Judge *is reading the paper.*

Rex
[not eagerly]

Well?

John

Well, of course, you realize that you're asking a great deal of me, Rex, but — [*Offers hand to* Rex *warmly.*] Be good to her, my boy, be good to her.

Rex
[shaking hands, forced warmth]

Thanks awfully. See-what-I-mean? [*To* Judge.] Congratulate me, Judge; I'm the happiest of men.

Judge
[looking up from newspaper]

So I see. Don't let it worry you.

> [Jean, *in riding costume, comes from the house.*

"And So They Were Married"

John
[*signalling* Judge *to leave*]
If Helen asks for me, I'm in the garden.

Judge
If any telegrams come for me, I'm writing to *my wife!*
[Jean *and* Rex *alone, they look at each other, not very loverlike.*

Jean
[*impulsively*]
You weren't in love with me yesterday. You aren't now. You would get out of it if you honorably could. But you honorably *can't!* So you have spoken to John; you are going to see it through, because you're a good sport. . . . I admire you for that, Rex, too much to hold you to it. You are released.

Rex
[*amazed*]
Why — why — you — you don't suppose I want to be released?

Jean
Well, I do! . . . Yesterday I let you pro-

pose to me when I cared for some one else. That's not fair to you, to me, to him!

REX
[*in a sudden fury*]
Who is he? What do you mean by this? Why didn't you tell me?

JEAN
I am telling you now. What have you ever told me about yourself?

REX
[*blinking*]
You had no right to play fast and loose with me.

JEAN
I'm making the only amends I can. You are free, I tell you.

REX
I don't want to be free! He can't have you! You are mine! If you think you can make me stop loving you ——

JEAN
[*interrupting*]
Love, Rex? Only jealousy. You've never been

in love with me — you've always been in love with Helen. But you couldn't get her, so you took me. Isn't that true, Rex?

REX

[*after an uncomfortable pause*]

I'll be honest with you, too. Yesterday I wasn't really very serious. I felt like a brute afterward. You tried your best to prevent what happened and ran away from me. But now ——

JEAN

Don't you know why I ran away? To make you follow. I made you catch me. I made you kiss me. Then you realized that we had been thrown together constantly — deliberately thrown together, if you care to know it — and, well, that's how many marriages are made. But I shan't marry on such terms. It's indecent!

REX

[*another pause*]

I never thought a *woman* could be capable of such honesty! . . . Oh, what a bully sport you are! You aren't like the rest that have been shoved at me. Why, I can respect you. You are the one for me.   [*He tries to take her.*

"And So They Were Married"

Jean

[*restraining him with dignity*]

I am sorry, Rex, but I am not for you.

Rex

Jean! without you . . . don't you see — I'll go straight to the devil!

Jean

That old, cowardly dodge? Any man who has no more backbone than that — why, I wouldn't marry you if you were the last man in the world.

Rex

[*frantic to possess what he cannot have*]

You won't, eh? We'll see about that. I want you now as I never wanted anything in my life, and I'll win you from him yet. You'll see!

[Helen *now appears.*

Helen

Oh, I beg your pardon. Lucy said John was out here.

Jean

I'll call him. [*She runs down into the garden.*

"And So They Were Married"

Rex

I'll call him.

[*He runs after* Jean. Helen *helplessly watches them go, sighs, standing by the garden steps until* John *ascends. He looks at* Helen *a moment, wondering how to begin. She looks so capable and unafraid of him.*]

John

If you hadn't gone to college, you could have done what Jean is doing.

Helen

[*with a shrug and a smile*]

But how proud you must be, John, to have a sister who isn't compelled to marry one man while in love with another. *Now,* aren't you glad I went to college?

[*She laughs good-naturedly at him.*]

John

Humph! If you think I'd let a sister of mine marry one of old man Baker's two-thousand-dollar employees ——

Helen

Why, John, didn't Ernest tell you? Doctor

"And So They Were Married"

Hawksbee has offered him a partnership. Just think of that!

John

What! Going back into private practice?

Helen

But it's such a fashionable practice. Hawksbee's made a million at it.

John

But the institute needs Hamilton.

Helen

Ah, but we need the money!

John
[disconcerted]

So you are going to spoil a noble career, are you? That's selfish. I didn't think it of you. There are thousands of successful physicians, but there is only one Ernest Hamilton.

Helen
[laughs]

Oh, don't worry, John, he has promised me to keep his two-thousand-dollar job.

"And So They Were Married"

John

Ah, I'm glad. You must let nothing interfere with his great humanitarian work. Think what it means to the lives of little children! Think what it means to the future of the race! Why, every one says his greatest usefulness has hardly begun!

Helen

Oh, I know all that, I've thought of all that.

John

Now, such men should be kept free from cares and anxiety. What was it you said yesterday? "He needs every cent of his salary for books, travel, all the advantages he simply must have for efficiency." To marry a poor man — most selfish thing a girl could do!

Helen

Yes, John, that's what I said yesterday.

John
[*scoring*]

But that was before he asked you! [Helen *smiles. He sneers.*] Rather pleased with yourself now, aren't you? "Just a woman after all"

"And So They Were Married"

— heroine of cheap magazine story! Sacrifices career for love! . . . All very pretty and romantic, my dear — but how about the man you love! Want to sacrifice his career, too?

Helen

But I'm not going to sacrifice what you are pleased to call my career. . . . Therefore he won't have to sacrifice his.

John

What! going to keep on working? Will he let the woman he loves work!

Helen
[*demure*]

Well, you see, he says I'm "too good" to loaf.

John

Humph! who'll take care of your home when you're at work? Who'll take care of your work when you're at home. Look at it practically. To maintain such a home as he needs on such a salary as he has — why, it would take all your time, all your energy. To keep him in his class you'll have to drop out of your own, become a household drudge, a servant.

"And So They Were Married"

Helen

And if I am willing?

John

Then where's your intellectual companionship? How'll you help his work? Expense for him, disillusionment for both. If you're the woman you pretend to be, you won't marry that man!

Helen

[*strong*]

The world needs his work, but he needs mine, and we both need each other.

John

[*stronger*]

And marriage would only handicap his work, ruin yours, and put you apart. You know that's true. You've seen it happen with others. You have told me so yourself!

Helen

Then that settles it! We must not, cannot, shall not marry. We have no right to marry. I agree with all you say — it would not join us together; it would put us asunder.

"And So They Were Married"

John
And you'll give him up? Good! Good!

Helen
Give him up? Never! The right to work, the right to love — those rights are inalienable. No, we'll give up marriage but not each other.

John
But — but — I don't understand.

Helen
[*straight in his eyes*]

We need each other — in our work and in our life — and we're to have each other — until life is ended and our work is done. Now, do you understand?

John
[*recoiling*]

Are you in your right mind? Think what you're saying.

Helen
I have thought all night, John. You have shown me how to say it.

"And So They Were Married"

John

But, but — why, this is utterly unbelievable! Why I'm not even shocked. Do you notice? I'm not even shocked? Because everything you have said, everything you have done — it all proves that you are a good woman.

Helen

If I were a bad woman, I'd inveigle him into marriage, John.

John

Inveigle! Marriage! Are you crazy? . . . Oh, this is all one of your highbrow jokes!

Helen

John, weren't you serious when you said marriage would destroy him?

John

But this would destroy *you!*

Helen

Well, even if that were so, which is more important to the world? Which is more important to your "great humanitarian work"?

"And So They Were Married"

John

Ah, very clever! A bluff to gain my consent to marrying him — a trick to get his salary raised.

Helen
[*with force*]

John, nothing you can do, nothing you can say, will ever gain my consent to marrying him. I've not told you half my reasons.

John

My God! my own sister! And did you, for one moment, dream that I would consent to that!

Helen

Not for one moment. I'm not asking your consent. I'm just telling you.

John
[*after scrutinizing her*]

Ridiculous! If you really meant to run away with this fellow, would you come and tell *me*, your own brother?

Helen

Do you suppose I'd *run* away without telling, even my own brother?

JOHN

[*looks at her a moment; she returns his gaze*]

Bah! — all pose and poppycock! [*He abruptly touches bell.*] I'll soon put a stop to this nonsense. [*Muttering.*] Damnedest thing I ever heard of.

HELEN

John, I understand exactly what I'm doing. You never will. But nothing *you* can do can stop me now.

JOHN

We'll see about that. [*The* BUTLER *appears.*] Ask the others to step out here at once; all except Miss Jean and Mr. Baker, I don't want them. Is Doctor Hamilton about?

BUTLER

No, sir, he went to church.

JOHN

All right. [*The* BUTLER *disappears.*] To church! My God!

> [HELEN *pays no attention. She gazes straight out into the future, head high, eyes clear and wide open.*

"And So They Were Married"

John

First of all, when the others come out, I'm going to ask them to look you in the face. Then you can make this statement to them, if you wish, and — look them in the face.

Helen
[*with quiet scorn*]

If I were being forced into such a marriage as poor little Jean's, I would kill myself. But in the eyes of God, who made love, no matter how I may appear in the eyes of man, who made marriage, I know that I am doing right.

[Lucy *comes out, followed by the* Judge.

John
[*not seeing them. He is loud*]

Say that to Uncle Everett and Cousin Theodore! Say that to my wife, stand up and say that to the world, if you dare.

Lucy
[*to* Judge]

She has told him!

"And So They Were Married"

JOHN
[*wheeling about*]
What! did she tell you? Why didn't you come to me at once?

LUCY
[*tremulous*]
She said she wanted to tell you herself. I didn't think she'd dare!

[*They all turn to look at* HELEN. THEODORE *comes back from church alone.*

HELEN
It had to be announced, of course.

THEODORE
[*advancing, beaming*]
Announced? What is announced?

[*All turn to him in a panic.*

LUCY
[*hurriedly*]
Their engagement, Theodore!

JUDGE
[*overriding* HELEN]
Yes, John has given his consent at last — example to society.   [*Prods* JOHN.

"And So They Were Married"

John
[*also overrides* Helen]

Of course! One of the finest fellows in the world.

Theodore
[*delighted*]

And withal he has a deep religious nature. Congratulations. My dear, he'll make an ideal husband.

[*Takes both* Helen's *hands, about to kiss her.*

Helen
[*can't help smiling*]

Thank you, cousin, but I don't want a husband. [*A sudden silence.*

Theodore
[*looks from one to the other*]

A lover's quarrel? — already!

Judge
[*enjoying it*]

No, Theodore, these lovers are in perfect accord. They both have conscientious scruples against marriage.

"And So They Were Married"

John
Conscientious!

Judge
So they are simply going to set up housekeeping without the mere formality of a wedding ceremony.   [Theodore *drops* Helen's *hands.*

Helen
[*quietly*]
We are going to do nothing of the sort.

Theodore
Uncle Everett!   [*Takes her hands again.*

Helen
We are not going to set up housekeeping at all. He will keep his present quarters and I mine.

John
But they are going to belong to each other.

Theodore
[*drops* Helen's *hands — aghast*]
I don't believe it.

"And So They Were Married"

Judge
[*apart to* Theodore]

The strike against marriage. It was bound to come.

Theodore
[*to* Judge]

But Church and State — [*indicates self and* Judge] must break this strike.

Helen

John is a practical man. He will prove to you that such a home as we could afford would only be a stumbling-block to Ernest's usefulness, a hollow sphere for mine. You can't fill it with mere happiness, Lucy, not for long, not for long.

Judge
[*restrains* Theodore *about to reply*]

Oh, let her get it all nicely talked out, then she'll take a nap and wake up feeling better. [*Whispering.*] We've driven her to this ourselves, but she really doesn't mean a word of it. Come, dear child, tell us all about this nightmare.

"And So They Were Married"

Helen
[*smiles at the* Judge]

Why, think what would happen to an eager intellect like Ernest Hamilton's if he had to come back to a narrow-minded apartment or a dreary suburb every evening and eat morbid meals opposite a housewife regaling him with the social ambitions of the other commuters. Ugh! It has ruined enough brilliant men already. [Judge *restrains* Theodore *and others who want to interrupt.*] Now at the University Club he dines, at slight expense compared with keeping up a home, upon the best food in the city with some of the best scientists in the country. . . . Marriage would divorce him from all that, would transplant him from an atmosphere of ideas into an atmosphere of worries. We should be forced into the same deadly ruts as the rest of you, uncle. Do you want me to destroy a great career, Theodore?

Theodore
Do you want to be a blot upon that career?

Helen
[*lightly*]

I'd rather be a blot than a blight, and that's what I'd be if I became his bride. Ask John.

"And So They Were Married"

Lucy

Do you want to be disgraced, despised, ostracized!

Helen

[*smiles at* Lucy]

A choice of evils, dear; of course, none of those costly well-kept wives on your visiting list will call upon me. But instead of one day at home, instead of making a tired husband work for me, I'll have all my days free to work with him, like the old-fashioned woman you admire! Instead of being an expense, I'll be a help to him; instead of being separated by marriage and divergent interests, we'll be united by love and common peril. . . . Isn't that the orthodox way to gain character, Theodore?

John

Oh, this is all damned nonsense! Look here, you've either got to marry this fellow now or else go away and never see him again; never, never!

Helen

Just what I thought, John. I intended never to see him again. That was why I let you send me abroad. But I'll never, never do it again.

"And So They Were Married"

[*Smiling like an engaged girl.*] It was perfectly dreadful! Ernest couldn't get along without me at all, poor old thing. And I, why, I nearly died.

John
Then you'll have to be married, that's all.

The Others
Why, of course you'll have to, that's all.

Helen
[*nodding*]

Oh, I know just how you feel about it. I thought so, too, at first, but I can't marry Ernest Hamilton. I love him.

Theodore
But if you love him truly — marriage, my dear, brings together those who love each other truly.

Helen
But those who love each other truly don't need anything to bring them together. The difficulty is to keep apart.

[*A reminiscent shudder.*

"And So They Were Married"

John

That's all romantic rot! Every one feels that way at first.

Helen

At first! Then the practical object of marriage is not to bring together those who love each other, but to keep together those who do not? [*To* Lucy.] What a dreadful thing marriage must be! [Judge *chokes down a chuckle.*

Judge

Ah, so you wish to be free to separate. Now we have it.

Helen

To separate? What an idea! On the contrary, we wish to be free to keep together! In the old days when they had interests in common marriage used to make man and woman one, but now it puts them apart. Can't you see it all about you? He goes down-town and works; she stays up-town and plays. He belongs to the laboring class; she belongs to the leisure class. At best, they seldom work at the same or similar trades. Legally it may be a union, but socially it's a mésalliance — in the eyes of God it's often worse. . . . No wonder that one in

"And So They Were Married"

eleven ends in divorce. The only way to avoid spiritual separation is to shun legal union like a contagious disease. Modern marriage *is* divorce. [*She turns to go, defiantly.*] I've found my work, I've found my mate, and so has he! What more can any human being ask?

[*The* BUTLER *appears.*

BUTLER
[*to* JOHN]

Doctor Hamilton is outside in a taxicab, sir.

JOHN

Show him here at once!

BUTLER

He says he does not care to come in, sir, unless you are ready to talk to him now.

JOHN

Well, of all the nerve! You bet I'm ready!

[*Starts off.* HELEN *starts, too.*

JUDGE
[*intercepting them calmly*]

Wait a minute — wait a minute. [*To* SERVANT.] Ask Doctor Hamilton kindly to wait in

"And So They Were Married"

the library. [*The* Butler *goes.*] Now, we're all a bit overwrought. [*Soothes* Helen, *pats her hand, puts arm about her, gradually leads her back.*] I still believe in you, Helen, I still believe in him. [*To all.*] It's simply that he's so deeply absorbed in his great work for mankind that he doesn't realize what he is asking Helen to do.

Helen
[*quietly*]

So I told him . . . when he asked me to marry him.

All

What! He *asked* you to *marry* him?

Helen

Of course! *Implored* me to marry him. [*She adds, smiling.*] So absorbed — not in mankind, but in me — that he "didn't realize what he was asking me to do."

Lucy
[*utterly amazed*]

And you refused him! The man who loves you honorably?

"And So They Were Married"

Helen
[*demurely*]

Of course! You don't suppose I'd take advantage of the poor fellow's weakness. Women often do, I admit — even when not in love, sometimes. . . . Not because they're depraved but dependent.

John
[*to all*]

And then he proposed this wicked substitute! Poisoned her innocent mind — the bounder!

Helen

But he did nothing of the sort.

John

Oh, your own idea, was it?

Helen

Of course!

John
[*to all*]

And he is willing to take advantage of the poor child's ignorance — the cad! [*To* Theodore.] "Deep religious nature," eh?

"And So They Were Married"

Theodore
I can't believe it of him.

Helen
He knows nothing about it yet. I haven't even seen him since I made my decision.

[*All exchange bewildered glances.*

John
[*apart to* Judge]

We've got to get him off to Paris. It's our only hope.

Judge
[*apart to* John]

You can't stop her following. She's on the edge of the precipice — do you want to shove her over? You are dealing with big people here and a big passion.   [*The* Butler *returns.*

Butler
Doctor Hamilton asks to see Miss Helen while waiting.

Judge
[*calmly to* Butler]

Tell Doctor Hamilton that Miss Helen will see him here.   [*The* Butler *leaves.*

"And So They Were Married"

John

Are you crazy! We've got to keep 'em apart — our one chance to save her.

Judge

No, bring them together. *That* is our one chance. Come, we'll go down into the garden and they'll have a nice little talk. Nothing like talk, John, honest talk, to clear these marriage problems. [*Going.*

John

And let them elope? In that taxicab? — not on your life! [*Runs to and fro.*

Judge

Come, John, girls never notify the family in advance when they plan elopements. It's not done.

Theodore
[*going*]

Uncle Everett is right. Ernest will bring her to her senses. He *has* a deep religious nature.

[Judge *leads* John *away to the garden.*

"And So They Were Married"

Lucy
[*lingering — to* Helen]

If you offer yourself on such terms to the man who loves you honorably, he'll never look at you again.

Theodore
[*leading* Lucy *off to garden*]

Don't worry! She won't.

[Ernest *rushes out to* Helen.

Helen

Ernest!

Ernest

At last! [*He takes her in his arms; she clings to him and gazes into his eyes; a long embrace.*] Tell me that you're all right again.

Helen
[*smiling with love and trust*]

Except that you deserted me, dear, just when I needed you most. Ernest, Ernest! never leave me again.

Ernest

Deserted you? Why, your brother said you were ill.

"And So They Were Married"

HELEN

Ah, I see . . . he was mistaken.

ERNEST

[*jubilant and boyish*]

But never mind now, I've got you at last, and I'll never, never let you go. You've got to sail with me to-morrow. Together! Oh, think! Together. [*Another embrace.*

HELEN

Are you *sure* you love me?

ERNEST

[*laughs from sheer joy of her nearness*]

Am I sure? Ten million times more to-day than yesterday.

HELEN

Even so . . . it is not, and can never be, as I love you.

ERNEST

[*with her hands in his, gayly*]

Then you can apologize.

HELEN

Apologize?

"AND SO THEY WERE MARRIED"

ERNEST

For saying, years and years ago — in other words, last night — that you didn't think you'd marry me after all. [*She starts.*] Why, what's the matter? You're trembling like a leaf. You *are* ill!

HELEN

No; oh, no.

ERNEST
[*tenderly*]

Still a few lingering doubts? I had hoped a good night's rest would put those little prejudices to sleep forever.

HELEN

Sleep?
[*She shakes her head, gazing at him soberly.*

ERNEST

So you could not sleep? Neither could I; I was too happy to sleep. I was afraid I'd miss some wondrous throbbing thought of your loveliness. [*Takes her passive hand, puts a kiss in it, and closes it reverently while she looks into his eyes without moving.*] Do you know, I'm disappointed in love. I always thought it meant soft sighs and pretty speeches. It means an agony of longing, delicious agony, but, oh, terrific. [*She says nothing.*] Dear, dear girl, it may be easy for you, but I can't stand much more of this.

HELEN

Nor I.

ERNEST

You must come to Paris with me or I'll stay home. All through the night I had waking visions of our being parted. Just when we had found each other at last. Some terrible impersonal monster stepped in between us and said: "No. Now that you have had your glimpse of heaven — away! Ye twain shall not enter here. . . ." Silly, wasn't it? But I couldn't get the horror of it out of my head.

HELEN

[*nodding*]

Do you know why, Ernest? Because it was in mine. It came from my thought to yours. You and I are attuned like wireless instruments. Even in the old blind days, there in the laboratory I used to read your mind. Shall I tell you

"And So They Were Married"

the name of the monster that would put us asunder? . . . Its name is Marriage.

Ernest

But I need you. You know that. And you need me. It's too late. We are helpless now — in the clutch of forces more potent than our little selves — forces that brought us into the world — forces that have made the world. Whether you will or no, this beautiful binding power is sweeping you and me together. And you must yield.

Helen

[reaching for his hand]

Ah, my dear, could anything make it more beautiful, more binding than it is now?

Ernest

It is perfect. The one divine thing we share with God. The Church is right in that respect. I used to look upon marriage as a mere contract. It's a religious sacrament.

Helen

Does the wedding ceremony make it sacred?

"And So They Were Married"

Ernest

That mediæval incantation! No, love, which is given by God, not the artificial form made by man.

Helen

I knew it! I knew you'd see it — the mistake of all the ages. They've tried to make love fit marriage. It can't be done. Marriage must be changed to fit love. [*Impulsively.*] Yes, I'll go to Paris with you.

Ernest
[*about to take her in his arms*]

You darling!

Helen
[*steps back*]

But not as your wife.

Ernest
[*stops — perplexed*]

You mean . . . without marriage?

Helen

I mean without marriage.

[*They look into each other's eyes.*

"And So They Were Married"

Ernest

A moment ago I thought I loved you as much as man could love woman. I was mistaken in you — I was mistaken in myself. For now I love you as man never loved before. You superb, you wonderful woman!

Helen

[*holds out her hand to be shaken, not caressed*]
Then you agree?

Ernest

[*kneels, kisses her hand, and arises*]
Of course not! You blessed girl, don't you suppose I understand? It's all for my sake. Therefore for your sake — no.

Helen

Then for my sake — for the sake of everything our love stands for!

Ernest

[*laughing fondly*]
Do you think I'd let you do anything for anybody's sake you're sure, later, to regret?

"And So They Were Married"

Helen

Then don't ask me to marry you, Ernest. We'd both regret that later. It would destroy the two things that have brought us together, love and work.

Ernest

Nonsense. Nothing could do that. . . . And besides, think of our poor horrified families! Think of the world's view!

Helen

Aren't we sacrificing enough for the world — money, comforts, even children? Must we also sacrifice each other to the world? Must we be hypocrites because others are? Must we, too, be cowards and take on the protective coloring of our species?

Ernest

Our ideas may be higher than society's, but society rewards and punishes its members according to its own ideas, not ours.

Helen

Do you want society's rewards? Do you fear society's punishment?

"And So They Were Married"

Ernest
[*jubilantly enfolding her*]

With you in my arms, I want nothing from heaven, I fear nothing from hell; but, my dear [*shrugs and comes down to earth with a smile and releases her*], consider the price, consider the price.

Helen

Aren't you willing to pay the price?

Ernest

I? Yes! But it's the woman, always the woman, who pays.

Helen

I am willing to pay.

Ernest

I am not willing to let you.

Helen

You'll have to be, dear. I shall go with you on my terms or not at all.

Ernest
[*with decision*]

You will come with me as my wife or stay at home.

"And So They Were Married"

Helen

[*gasping*]

Now? After all I've said, all I've done? Ernest: I've told the family! I relied upon you. I took for granted — Ernest, you wouldn't — you couldn't leave me behind now.

Ernest

Thanks to you and what you've made of me, I must and will.

Helen

Ernest! [*Opens her arms to him to take her.*

Ernest

[*about to enfold her — resists*]

No! If you love me enough for that [*points to her pleading hands*] — I love you enough for this. [*He turns to go.*] Come when you're ready to marry me.

Helen

[*shrill, excited, angered*]

Do you think this has been easy for me? Do you think I'll offer myself again on any terms? Never!

"And So They Were Married"

Ernest

You must marry me — and you will.

Helen

You don't know me. Good-by!

Ernest

Very well!

[Ernest, *afraid to stay, goes at once. She waits motionless until she hears the automobile carrying him away. She immediately turns from stone to tears, with a low wail. In utter despair, hands outstretched she sinks down upon a bench and buries her face in her hands.*

Helen

Oh, Ernest! . . . How could you?

[Lucy, Theodore, Judge *and* John *all hurry back, all excited.*

Theodore

Did you see his horrified look?

Lucy

Fairly running away — revolted. Ah!

[*Points at* Helen. Helen *arises, defiant, confident, calm.*

"And So They Were Married"

John
[*to* Helen]

What did I tell you!

Lucy

You have thrown away the love of an honorable man.

Theodore

Trampled upon the finest feelings of a deep nature.

John

Let this be a lesson to you. You've lost your chance to marry, your chance to work, and now, by heavens! you will cut out "independence" and stay at home, *where women belong*, and live down this disgrace . . . if you can.

Lucy

With one excuse or another — he'll stay away. He'll never come back.

Helen
[*clear and confident as if clairvoyant*]

He will! He is coming now. . . . He is

"And So They Were Married"

crossing the hall. . . . He is passing through the library. . . . He's here!

[*But she doesn't turn.* ERNEST *reappears at the door and takes in the situation at a glance.*

JOHN
[*still turned toward* HELEN]

He'll never look at you again, and I don't blame him! I'm a man; I know. We don't respect women who sell out so cheap.

ERNEST

You lie! [*All turn, astounded.* HELEN *runs toward* ERNEST *with a cry of joy.* JOHN *starts to block her. To* JOHN.] Stop! You're not fit to touch her. No man is.

JOHN
[*with a sarcastic laugh*]

Humph! I suppose that's why you ran away.

ERNEST

Yes. To protect her from myself.

JOHN

Then why come back?

"And So They Were Married"

Ernest

To protect her from you! You cowards, you hypocrites! [*He rushes down to* Helen, *puts his strong arm about shoulder and whispers rapidly.*] Just as I started, something stopped me. In a flash I saw . . . all this.

Helen
[*clasping his arm with both hands*]

I made you come! I made you see!

John
[*advances menacingly*]

By what right are you here in my home? By what right do you take my sister in your arms?

Ernest

By a right more ancient than man-made law! I have come to the cry of my mate. I'm here to fight for the woman I love! [*Arm about* Helen, *defies the world. To all.*] My trip to Paris is postponed. One week from to-day gather all your family here, and in your home we'll make our declaration to the world.

John

In my home! Ha! Not if I know it.

"And So They Were Married"

Judge
[*restraining* John]

Play for time, John — he'll bring her around.

John
[*to* Ernest]

Do you mean to marry her or not? Speak my language!

> [Ernest *releases* Helen *and steps across to* John.

Ernest

She decides that — not you.

> [*All turn to* Helen.

Helen

Never!

John
[*shaking off* Judge. *To* Helen.]

You'll go with this damned fanatic only over my dead body.

Helen
[*high*]

And that will only cry aloud the thing you wish to hide from the world you fear.

> [*Just now* Jean *is seen slowly returning from the garden without* Rex. *Her pretty*

"And So They Were Married"

head is bent and, busy with her own sad thoughts, she is startled by the following:

Ernest

There are laws to prevent marriage in some cases but none to enforce marriage on women — unless they will it.

John
[*beside himself with rage*]

Enforce! Do you think I'll ever *allow* a sister of mine to marry a libertine?

Jean
[*thinks they are discussing her, and is outraged*]

But I'm not going to marry him! My engagement is broken.

[*General consternation. Sobbing,* Jean *runs into house.*

John

My God, what next? Lucy, don't let Rex get away! You know what he'll do — and when he sobers up, it may be too late. [*To* Ernest.] As for *you*, you snake, you get right out of here.

"And So They Were Married"

Judge
[*in the sudden silence*]
Now you've done it, John.

Ernest
Oh, very well, this is your property.

Helen
But *I* am not! I go, too!
[*She runs to* Ernest.

Theodore
Don't commit this sin!

John
Let her go! She's no sister of mine.

Judge
[*the only calm one*]
If she leaves this house now, it's all up.

John
A woman who will give herself to a man without marriage is no sister of mine.

"And So They Were Married"

Helen

[*about to go, turns, leaning on* Ernest. *To all*]

Give! . . . But if I *sold* myself, as you are forcing poor little Jean to do, to a libertine she does not love, who does not love her — that is not sin! That is respectability! To urge and aid her to entrap a man into marriage by playing the shameless tricks of the only trade men want women to learn — that is holy matrimony. But to give yourself of your own free will to the man you love and trust and can help, the man who loves and needs and has won the right to have you — oh, if this is sin, then let me live and die a sinner!

> [*She turns to* Ernest, *gives him a look of complete love and trust, then bursts into tears upon his shoulder, his arms enfolding her protectingly.*

Act III

Act III

It is well along in the afternoon of the same busy day of rest. Most unaccountably — until the Judge *accounts for it later — the terrace has been decked out with festoons and flowers since the excitement of the morning. Japanese lanterns have been hung, though it is not yet time to light them and though it is Sunday in a pious household.*
Most incongruously and lugubriously, Lucy *is pacing to and fro in silent concern.*
Theodore *now comes out of the house, also looking harassed.* Lucy *turns to him inquiringly. He shakes his head sadly.*

Lucy

NO word from Uncle Everett?

Theodore

No word. He must have reached town long ago, unless he had tire trouble. . . . It's a bad sign, Lucy, a bad sign. He would surely telephone us.

"And So They Were Married"

Lucy

Oh, if he *only* hadn't missed their train!

Theodore

[*hopelessly*]

Uncle Everett is the only one who could have brought them to their senses.

Lucy

It may not be too late. He took our fastest car, our best chauffeur.

Theodore

Detectives are to watch all the steamers tomorrow. John telephoned at once.

Lucy

But to-morrow will be too late! And, oh! when it all comes out in the newspapers! The ghastly head-lines — "well-known scientist, beautiful daughter of a prominent family!" Oh! What will people say?

[John, *hurried and worried, rushes out shouting for* Lucy.

John

Any news? Any news? [Theodore *and* Lucy

"And So They Were Married"

give him gestures of despair.] Then it's too late. [*He, too, paces to and fro in fury. Then bracing up.*] Well, I found Rex, over at the Golf Club. Terribly cut up. But listen; not a drink, not one! . . . Where's Jean? Got to see her at once.

Theodore

Locked herself up in her room, John, crying her little heart out!

John

Rex is a changed man, I tell you. We've got to patch it up, and we've got to do it *quick!*

Lucy

But, John! When the Bakers hear about Helen . . . Rex marry into our family? Never! We're disgraced, John, disgraced!

John
[*impatiently*]

But they're not *going* to hear about Helen. No one knows, and no one *will*. Helen has simply returned to Paris to complete her scientific research. My press-agent — he's attending to all that.

"And So They Were Married"

THEODORE

But questions, gossip, rumor — it's bound to come out in time!

JOHN

In time; but meanwhile, if Jean marries Rex, the Bakers will *have* to stand for it. What's more, they'll make *other* people stand for it. Backed by the Bakers, no one will *dare* turn us down. . . . Our position in the world, my business relations with the old man — *everything hangs on little Jean* now. Tell her I've simply got to see her. [LUCY *hesitates*.] Hurry! Rex is coming over later. [*He catches sight of the table, festoons, etc.*] Heavens! What's all this tomfoolery?

LUCY
[*going*]

Uncle Everett's orders — he wouldn't stop to explain. He left word to summon the whole family for dinner.   [LUCY *goes.*

JOHN
[*shrilly*]

The whole family! . . . To-day of all days!

"And So They Were Married"

THEODORE

John! You must not, shall not, force Jean to marry this man.

JOHN
[*unappreciated*]

Haven't I done everything for my sisters? Can't they even *marry* for *me*?

THEODORE

The man she loves or none at all.

JOHN

That cub at the law school? No money to keep a wife, no prospects of any. His father's a college professor.

THEODORE
[*shaking head sadly*]

"No love without marriage, no marriage without — money!" Ernest Hamilton's words this morning, when we walked to church.

JOHN
[*watching house expectantly*]

Survival of the fittest, Theodore, survival of the fittest.

"And So They Were Married"

Theodore

The fittest for what? — for making money! the only kind of fitness encouraged to survive, to reproduce its species.

John

If the ability to make money is not the test of fitness, what is?

Theodore

Then you are more fit than a hundred Hamiltons, are you? And Rex? How fit is he? Rex never made a cent in his life.

John

He's got it, all the same. . . . See here! Haven't I enough to worry me without *your* butting in? Jean's got to marry *some*body, *some*time, hasn't she?

Theodore

But not Rex, not if I can prevent it.

John

But you can't — you have nothing to do with it . . . except to perform the ceremony and get a big, fat fee for it.

"And So They Were Married"

Theodore

I — marry Jean and Rex? Never!

> [Jean *comes out. She is frightened and turns timidly to* Theodore *for protection.*

John

Jean, don't detain Theodore. He has an important business letter to write. [Theodore *turns to* John *indignantly.*] Your wife's sanatorium bills — better settle up before they dun you again.

Theodore

With your money?

> [*Takes* John's *check out of pocket, about to tear it.*

John

> [*catching* Theodore's *hand*]

For Mary's sake, for the children's — don't give way to selfish pride. . . . Want to kill your wife? Then take her out of the sanatorium. Want to ruin your children? Then take them out of school! . . . Cash your check, I tell you, and pay your debts!

> [Theodore *glances at* Jean, *at check. A struggle. At bay, he finally pockets check and dejectedly goes into the house.*

"And So They Were Married"

Jean

[*with a wet handkerchief in hand*]

Well? If I refuse to marry Rex? . . . Cut off my allowance or merely bully me to death?

John

[*kindly*]

Oh, come! You've filled your romantic little head full of novels. I never force *anybody* to do *anything*. [*Suddenly breaks out.*] My heavens! what's the matter with all of you? I only want to give you and Lucy and Helen and Theodore and the whole family the best of everything in life! And what do I get for it? I'm a brutal husband, a bullying brother, and a malefactor of wealth. Lord! I guess I have some rights, even if I have got money!

Jean

Rex has money, too. Should that give him the right to women? I, too, have some rights — even though I *am* a woman.

John

Any woman who can't care enough for a Baker to marry him — Rex is the sort who

"And So They Were Married"

would do everything in the world for the woman he loves, everything. All the Bakers are like that.

JEAN

But what would he do for the woman he no longer loves?

JOHN

He wasn't fool enough to tell you about that?

JEAN

About what?

JOHN
[*halting*]

Nothing — I thought — I tell you, Rex has reformed.

JEAN

You thought I meant his "past." I meant his future . . . and my own.

JOHN

Well, if you expect to find a saint, you'll never get married at all.

JEAN

And if I never married at all?

"And So They Were Married"

John

Then what will you do?

Jean

[*with a wail of despair*]

That's it — then what *should* I do — what *could* I do? Oh, it's so unfair, so unfair to train girls only for this! What chance, what choice have I? To live on the bounty of a disapproving brother or a man I do not love! Oh, how I envy Helen! If I only had a chance, a decent chance!

John

Any sensible girl would envy your chance. You'll never have another like it. You'll never have another at all! Grab it, I tell you, grab it. [Rex *comes quietly, a determined look on his face,* John *sees him.*] Now, think, before too late, think hard. Think what it means to be an old maid. [*And leaves them abruptly.*

[Jean *stands alone, looking very pretty in girlish distress.* Rex *gazes at her a moment and then with sudden passion he silently rushes over, seizes her in his arms, kisses her furiously.*

"And So They Were Married"

JEAN

[*indignant, struggles, frees herself, and rubs her cheek*]

Ugh! How could you!

REX

Because I love you!

JEAN

Love! It isn't even respect now.

REX

Has that fellow ever kissed you?

JEAN

I have begged you never to refer to him again.

REX

He has! He has held you in his arms. He has kissed your lips, your cheeks, your eyes!

JEAN

How many women have you held in your arms? Have I ever tried to find out?

REX

Ah! You don't deny it, you can't.

"And So They Were Married"

Jean

I can! *He* respects me. I don't deserve it, but he does.

Rex

Thank heavens! Oh, you don't know how this has tormented me, little Jean. The thought of any other man's coming near you — why, I couldn't have felt the same toward you again, I just couldn't.

Jean
[*bites her lips — then deliberately*]

Well, then . . . other men have come near me . . . other men have kissed me, Rex.

Rex
[*getting wild again*]

What! When? Where?

Jean
[*laughing cynically*]

Oh, in conservatories in town, John's camp in the North Woods, motor rides in the country — once or twice out here on this very terrace, when I've felt sentimental in the moonlight.

"And So They Were Married"

Rex
[*recoiling*]

Oh! Jean! I never supposed *you* were that sort!

Jean
[*with distaste*]

Oh, I don't make a habit of it! I'm not *that* sort. But . . . well, this isn't all I could tell you about myself, Rex.

Rex

Don't! . . . Oh, what do you mean — quick.

Jean

Oh, I've merely been handled, not hurt. Slightly shop-worn but as good as new.

Rex
[*after a pause, quietly*]

Jean, what makes you say such horribly honest things to me?

Jean

Yesterday I did you a great unkindness, Rex. I deserve to suffer for it. . . . You don't suppose I enjoy talking this way about myself?

"And So They Were Married"

REX

I never heard a girl — a nice girl — talk like this before.

JEAN

Naturally not. Usually "nice" girls hide it. It's an instinct in women — to keep up their value. . . . Often I've had thoughts and feelings which "nice" girls of your artificial ideal are supposed never to have at all. Perfectly natural, too, especially girls of my sort. We have so little to occupy our minds, except men! To have a useful, absorbing occupation — it rubs off the bloom, lowers our price in the market, you see.

REX

Oh, stop! . . . If you're not going to marry me, say so, but ——

JEAN

But I am! . . . I am not going to be a dependent old maid. [REX, *bewildered, only gazes at her.*] But, first, I want you to know exactly what you're getting for your money. That seems only businesslike.

REX

[*recoils*]

Would you only marry me for that?

"And So They Were Married"

JEAN

I told you I loved another man. Do you want me?

REX

[*with jealousy returning*]

Do I want you! He shan't have you.

[*He comes close.*

JEAN

Then take me.

REX

[*seizes her passionately*]

I'll make you love *me!* [*Kisses her triumphantly.*] I'll bring a different light into those cold eyes of yours. Wait until you're married! Wait until you're awakened. I'll make you forget that man, all other men. You are to be mine — all mine, all mine! [*During this embrace* JEAN *is quite passive, holds up her cheek to be kissed, and when he seeks her lips she shuts her eyes and gives him her lips. He suddenly stops, chilled; holding her at arm's length.*] But I don't care to marry an iceberg. Can't you love me a little? Haven't you any sentiment in your cynical little soul . . . .you irresistible darling!

"And So They Were Married"

Jean

In my soul? Yes! It's only my body I'm selling, you know.

[*Then deliberately — clearly without passion — throws her arms about his neck, clinging close and kissing him repeatedly until* Rex *responds.*

Rex

Look out, here comes the parson.

[Theodore *comes out of the house.*

Jean

Oh, Theodore! Rex and I have come to an understanding. . . . Will you solemnize our blessed union?

Theodore

Not unless you truly love each other. Marriage is sacred.

Jean

[*rapidly*]

A large church wedding — that will make it sacred. A full choral service — many expensive flowers — all the smartest people invited — that always makes the union of two souls sacred.

"And So They Were Married"

Theodore

Those who truly love — their friends should witness the solemn rite, but ——

Jean

[*interrupts. To* Rex]

And my wedding gown will be white satin with a point-lace veil caught up with orange-blossoms and a diamond tiara — "the gift of the groom" — that ought to make it solemn.

Theodore

The white veil is the symbol of purity, Jean.

Jean

[*rattling on wildly*]

Of purity, Rex, do you hear? Whenever you see a bride in the white symbol of purity she is pure — that proves it. That makes it all so beautiful! so sacred! so holy! holy! holy!

[*Hysterically turns and runs into the house as* John *comes out.*

Theodore

[*following*]

Jean, you must not, you shall not — [John *blocks* Theodore. Rex *runs in after* Jean. *To*

"And So They Were Married"

JOHN.] John, I warn you! I'll prevent this marriage. I'll tell every clergyman in the diocese. I'll inform the bishop himself. This marriage would be a sacrilege.

JOHN

You dare threaten me — after all I've done for you!

THEODORE

Your five thousand was a loan — not a bribe — every cent of it will be returned.

JOHN

You can't return it. I wouldn't let you if you could. Come, it's all in the family. [THEODORE shakes his head.] You know that beautiful Gothic chapel old man Baker is building on his estate? He likes you. I'll tell him you're just the man he's looking for — safe and sane — no socialistic tendencies.

THEODORE

Don't trouble yourself — he offered me the place this morning.

JOHN

You didn't refuse it!

"And So They Were Married"

Theodore

I did — this morning. But since my last talk with you I've reconsidered, I've telephoned my acceptance.

John
[*genuinely glad*]

Bully! Great! Why, now you're fixed for life. "Only one kind of fitness encouraged," eh? . . . Right always triumphs in the end. Never lose your faith again, Theodore.

Theodore

Right? That whited sepulchre! his mill hands dying like flies, his private life a public scandal!

John
[*with a cynical grin*]

Then why accept his tainted money?

Theodore
[*from his soul*]

To keep my wife alive. To keep my children out of the streets. To keep myself out of deeper debt to you. That's why I accept it — that's why many a man sells his soul to the devil. . . . If I had only myself to consider — why, to me a

"And So They Were Married"

little thing like death would be a blessed luxury. But I, why, John, I cannot afford — even to die. I must compromise and live — live for those dependent on me. . . . Your five thousand will be returned with interest, but your little sister will not be married to a man she does not want.

John

But Rex wants *her* and money talks in this world, louder than the Church. Refuse to marry Baker's son and how long will you keep Baker's chapel? . . . Think it over, Theodore, think it over.

> [*Suddenly the* Judge *in motor garments covered with dust comes out panting, followed by* Lucy *calling.*]

Lucy

Uncle Everett! Uncle Everett!

Judge

John! Oh, John!

John

Where is she!

"And So They Were Married"

Theodore
You were too late!

Judge
Wait! Give me time to get my breath.
[*Fans himself with his cap and mops brow.*

John
My detective — didn't he meet their train?
[Judge *nods yes.*

Lucy
But they saw him first?
[Judge *shakes head no.*

Theodore
Didn't he follow them? [Judge *nods yes.*

John
Where'd they go? Where are they? Speak, man, speak!

Judge
[*raises cap and handkerchief*]
Now, just give me a chance and I'll tell the whole story. . . . The detective was waiting

"And So They Were Married"

at the station. He saw them step out of the train. He followed them to the cab-stand. He watched them get into a taxi — jumped into another himself — and away they went, pursued by the detective and blissfully ignorant of his existence. . . . Even now they don't know they were being watched — or else . . . well, they might have taken another course.

Lucy
Quick! Tell us the worst.

Judge
[*hesitates*]
Well . . . they drove straight to Helen's apartment.

Lucy
And you were too late. I thought so.

John
But my detective?

Judge
He followed and reported to me when I reached town.

"AND SO THEY WERE MARRIED"

LUCY

Reported what? Tell us all.

JUDGE

First he saw Ernest help Helen out of the taxi — very tenderly, like this. Little they realized then how every detail was to be reported to you now!

JOHN

Go on! Go on!

JUDGE

Then the detective saw Ernest deliberately ——

LUCY

Yes, go on.

JUDGE

Deliberately lift his hat like this, say "good afternoon" just like that, and drive on to his own apartment a mile away.

[*There is a sudden silence; the others waiting the* JUDGE *now sits down.*]

LUCY

Oh, is that all?

"And So They Were Married"

Theodore
Why, it's exactly as if they were engaged!

Judge
No, Theodore, not *exactly* as if engaged.

John
You're keeping something back from us! Speak!

Judge
[*gets up from chair*]

Must I tell you? It's rather delicate. . . . Well, he didn't even step into the vestibule to kiss her good-by.   [*All look at each other.*

John
But where are they now? Quick!

Lucy
They met later! I knew it.

Judge
Yes, it's true. They are alone together at this very moment.

"And So They Were Married"

All
Where! Where?

Judge
[*pointing to house*]
There.

John
What! What are they doing here?

Judge
[*resumes fanning*]
Discussing the marriage problem. [*General rejoicing and relief.*] Sssh! Not so loud, you might interrupt them.

John
[*nodding knowingly*]
Cold feet! Knew he'd lose his job.

Lucy
The disgrace. She couldn't face it.

Theodore
No, conscience. A deep religious nature.
  [*They all think it over a moment, each sure of his own diagnosis.*

"And So They Were Married"

JOHN
[*turning to* JUDGE *with amusement*]
So! Decided the soul-mate theory wouldn't work in practice, eh?

THEODORE *and* LUCY
And they agree to marry?

JUDGE
[*stops fanning*]
Marry? My, no! Nothing like that. They think less of marriage than ever now! Helen is using woman's sweet indirect influence on Ernest in there at this moment!
[*All start toward the house impulsively, but on second thoughts they all stop.*

JOHN
Then how on earth did you get them back!

JUDGE
[*lighting cigar*]
Oh, perfectly simple, I promised Helen you'd apologize to Ernest; promised Ernest you'd apologize to Helen. [*To* LUCY.] Promised both you'd arrange a nice little family party for 'em. They bear no grudge. They're too happy.

"And So They Were Married"

LUCY
[*horrified. Indicates table*]
The family party — for *them*? Horrors!

JUDGE
[*tossing away match*]
Yes, here in your happy home. [*The others turn on the* JUDGE *indignantly.*] Well, don't jump on *me*. I tell you they positively decline to elope until after they tell the whole damn family. Considerate of them, I say. You don't deserve it, if you ask me.

JOHN
[*incredulous*]
Tell the whole. . . see here, are they crazy? Are *you* crazy? Do you think *I'm* crazy?
[*Impetuously turns toward the house, a man of action.*

JUDGE
[*stopping* JOHN]
Wait! . . . You've already done your best to destroy your sister — but you've utterly failed. They have done nothing wrong — *as yet*. Why, they are the finest, truest, noblest pair of lovers I ever met! Now, aren't they, Theodore?

"And So They Were Married"

Theodore

I can't say that I call Helen's ideas of marriage "noble," exactly!

Judge
[*grandiloquent*]

She is willing to sacrifice even marriage for his career. Isn't that noble? And he! willing to sacrifice even his career for marriage. Both noble, if you ask me.

John
[*loud*]

Noble tommy-rot! — a pair of pig-headed, highbrow fools! They don't have to sacrifice anything for anybody. Can't they work together just as well married as unmarried?

Judge
[*slyly*]

That's what I said to her, but you had already convinced her that it was impractical. Work and marriage — "combine the two, and you'll fail at both" — your own warning, John.

John
[*angry*]

B'r'r — you think you're very funny, don't

"And So They Were Married"

you! But that's my sister in there, planning to be that fellow's mistress — right here in my own house! Anything funny about that!

JUDGE
[*stepping aside*]

All right, go put a stop to it then! [JOHN *starts toward house.*] It's your own house — turn her out again. [JOHN *stops short.*] What are you going to do about it, John? [JOHN *has no answer.*] Drive little Jean into marriage with a man she does not love — she is an old-fashioned girl. But your other sister — you can't make her marry even the man she does love, unless she sees fit. She is the New Woman! Society can no longer force females into wedlock — so it is forcing them out . . . by the thousands! Approve of it? Of course not. But what good will our disapproval do? They will only laugh at you. The strike is on. Few of the strikers will let you see it. Few of the strikers have Helen's courage. But, believe it or not, the strike will spread. It cannot be crushed by law or force. Unless society wakes up and reforms its rules and regulations of marriage, marriage is doomed. . . . What are you going to do about it? [*Silence.*] I thought so — nothing. Call them bad women and let it go at that. Blame it all on human nature, made by God, and leave untouched our human institutions, made by man. You poor little pessimists! human nature to-day is better than it ever was, but our most important institution is worse — the most sacred relationship in life has become a jest in the market-place. . . . You funny little cowards, you're afraid of life, afraid of love, afraid of truth. You worship lies, and call it God!

John
[*interrupts*]

All right, all right — but we can't change marriage overnight just to suit Helen. What are *you* going to do about it?

Judge

There's just one thing to do. Will you back me up in everything I say?

John
[*acknowledging his own defeat*]

Anything — everything.

Judge

Then tell Helen she doesn't have to marry,

that, with the best intentions, the Church has made a muddle of monogamy.

THEODORE
Uncle Everett, I protest.

JUDGE
That we all admire their consecrated courage and advise their trying this conscientious experiment.

JOHN
Not if I have anything to say about it!

JUDGE
But you haven't. Do please get that through your head. . . . Theodore, they've talked enough, ask them to step out here and receive John's blessing. [*Impatiently.*] Go on — I'll fix John. [THEODORE *goes.*] [*To* JOHN, *who is about to burst forth.*] Oh, see here, did you ever pull a dog into the house against his will? . . . Let him alone and he'll follow you in, wag his tail, and lick your hand.

JOHN
You mean, they'll come in, be respectable?

"And So They Were Married"

JUDGE

Admit that marriage has numerous drawbacks — and they'll see its advantages. Deny it — and they'll see nothing but each other. Marriage *is* in a bad way, but it's the less of two evils. Marriage *must* adjust itself to the New Woman — *but* the New Woman must meanwhile adjust herself to marriage. [*Briskly to* LUCY.] Now, then, did you send out that hurry call for the family this evening?

LUCY

Yes, they're on their way here now, but Uncle Everett, Doctor Hamilton said, next week.

JUDGE

Yes, I know — it'll be a little surprise party for Helen. . . . Did you order some music?

LUCY

Yes, the musicians are to be stationed in the library.

JUDGE

Excellent, excellent. [*Indicates tables and festoons.*] All that junk will help, too. A good Sunday supper this evening, Lucy; your best champagne, John — gay spirits, family affection, warm approval, toasts to the future. Why, all we'll have to do is — [*Breaks off.*] Here they come. Now follow my lead. They've done a lot of thinking since you saw them last, but — make one misstep and it's all off.

Lucy

Be nice to her, John. It was just a girlish impulse.

[J OHN *opens arms to receive* H ELEN.

John

My sister! All is forgiven.

Helen

[*stops short, her lip curls*]
You forgive *me?*

[*Before* J OHN *can reply,* T HEODORE *and* E RNEST *follow, talking.*

Ernest

But I tell you he had a perfect right to put me off his property. The thing I can't overlook — [*Sees* J OHN *and* L UCY *. Points finger at them*

"And So They Were Married"

accusingly.] Theodore has told me what you thought. . . . Please don't judge us by yourselves again — you licentious-minded married people!

[*He shrugs his shoulders with fastidious disgust and turns his back upon them.*

John
[*gasping*]
Well, I'll be damned.

Judge
[*whispers*]
Stand for it — he's right.

Theodore
But Ernest . . . I'm bound to say when two people run away together ——

Ernest
Ah, Theodore! you, too? Are all married people alike? Did we want to "run away" as you call it? Did we not ask for a week to think it over? Did we not stipulate that in any case we must frankly face the family first? But this person — what did he do? he ordered us off

"And So They Were Married"

his property, like trespassers! What could we do? Sit down in the road and wait a week? Bah! we went home — you suspicious married people, you hypocritical, unspeakable married people! [JUDGE *has difficulty in restraining* JOHN.] Why, I believe our good friend the Judge here is the only decent-minded, properly married person on your property.

JOHN
[*bursting out*]
Decent-minded — why, he's div ——
[LUCY *stops him.*

JUDGE
[*steps in*]
Dev-oted to his wife. Lucy is jealous of what I'm doing for my wife. [*Controls laughter.*] Now come, we must all just let bygones be bygones. We know your intentions are honorable, your courage admirable; and for whatever was amiss in word, deed, or thought, we all humbly apologize — don't we, John? [JOHN *bows uncomfortably.*] Lucy? Theodore? And now I want you all to tell Ernest and Helen what you told me — that their arguments against marriage are unanswerable, their logic unimpeachable, and we

"And So They Were Married"

no longer have the slightest intention or desire to get them divorced by matrimony. [JOHN, THEODORE, *and* LUCY *look dubious.* JUDGE *crosses over and pinches them.* HELEN *and* ERNEST *are utterly bewildered.*] Why, we wouldn't let a little thing like marriage come between them for the world, would we, John? would we, Lucy? would we, Theodore?

JOHN
[*with an effort*]
I agree with Uncle Everett entirely.

JUDGE
And you, Theodore?

THEODORE
[*in a low voice*]
Perfectly.

JUDGE
And you, Lucy?

LUCY
[*with a nervous glance at* JOHN]
Absolutely.

"And So They Were Married"

JUDGE
[*to the lovers*]
There. You see?
[ERNEST *looks from one to the other in amazement.*

HELEN
[*laughing*]
I don't believe a word of it!

JUDGE
Why not? why not?

HELEN
Very well, then invite the whole family here next Sunday!

JUDGE
They'll be here in an hour.   [*Points to tables.*

HELEN *and* ERNEST
[*recoiling*]
In an hour!

JUDGE
Yes, you are to begin your new life together this evening! Isn't it lovely?

"And So They Were Married"

Helen
[*gasping*]

But that's so sudden. Why, we — we aren't ready.

Theodore
Just as ready as you'll ever be.

Judge
Ernest's vacation begins to-morrow — your honeymoon.

Helen
But, don't you see ——

Lucy
Those new Paris clothes John gave you — your trousseau.

Ernest
Well, but ——

Judge
And this family gathering this evening, your — in a manner of speaking — wedding party. [*Waving aside all the lovers' objections.*] Now, it's all fixed, let's go and dress for the — as it were — ceremony.

"And So They Were Married"

Ernest
[*blocks the way. Serious*]

Wait! Did I ever say I would not marry this woman? [*All stop, turn, exchange glances.*

Judge
[*apart*]

Ah! a broad-minded chap.

John
[*with a wink at* Judge]

Ah! so you think you'd like to marry my sister after all?

Ernest

Oh, you're an ass! What have I been doing for the past twenty-four hours? Begging her to marry me. What have you been doing? Preventing it. Why did I postpone sailing for a week? Why did I insist upon the family party? [*Comes nearer to* John.] You're an idiot.

Judge
[*pinching* John]

Stand for it, John. You've got to stand for it. Tell him you love him like a brother . . . in-law.

"And So They Were Married"

John
[*controls himself*]

Well, I . . . I — you have my consent, Doctor Hamilton, I'm sure.

Ernest

Your consent! What's that got to do with it? [*They all turn toward* HELEN. ERNEST *steps between them.*] Now wait! . . . This morning you tried bullying. Did it work? This afternoon bluffing. Think *that* will work? [*Hand on* HELEN's *shoulder.*] You can't frighten her into marriage. I've tried that myself. We've got to appeal to some higher motive than self-interest or superstition with *this* woman, racial motives, unselfish motives. [*With force.*] But don't talk to me about her being "immoral." I won't stand for it. If you want her to marry, prove the morality of marriage.

Theodore

The "morality of marriage"! What next?

Ernest
[*to* THEODORE]

That's what I said — the morality of *marriage!* This woman is not on trial before you.

"And So They Were Married"

Marriage is on trial before her, and thus far I'm bound to say you've not made out a good case for it. But simply *justify* her marrying me, and — I give you my word — you can perform the ceremony this very evening. No license is required in this State, you know.

[*This creates a sensation.*

Judge

Now, what could be fairer than that! [*To* Helen.] Do you agree to this?

Helen
[*she nods*]

We agree in everything.

Judge

Both broad-minded!

Helen
[*quietly*]

I never said I did not believe in a legal wedding — [*others surprised*] for those who can afford the luxury of children. . . . But for those who have to take it out in working for other people's children all their lives — a ceremony seems like a subterfuge. Without children I don't see how any marriage is ever consummated — socially.

THEODORE

Ah, but this relationship — it's a sacred thing in itself.

HELEN

[*sincerely*]

I know it. I want to do right, Theodore, please believe that I do! But the kind of marriage preached by the Church and practised by the world — does that cherish the real sacredness of this relationship? Of course, I can only judge from appearances, but so often marriage seems to destroy the sacredness — yes, and also the usefulness — of this relationship!

ERNEST

But, my dear girl ——

HELEN

[*smiles*]

He thinks so, too. Only he has a quaint, mannish notion that he must "protect me." [*To* ERNEST, *patting his arm.*] Haven't you, dear!

[*Again she has raised the shield of flippancy.*

"And So They Were Married"

Judge

What did I tell you, Theodore? The old marriage doesn't fit the New Woman. A self-supporting girl like Helen objects to obeying a mere man — like Ernest.

Helen

[*patting the* Judge's *arm affectionately, too*]

Uncle Everett, you know nothing about it! You think you understand the new generation. The only generation you understand is the one which clamored for "Woman's Rights." [*To* Ernest.] I obey you already — every day of my life, do I not, dear? [*Looking up into his face.*] You're my "boss," aren't you, Ernest? [*To* Judge.] But I do object to contracting by law for what is better done by love.

Judge
[*laughs fondly*]

But suppose the promise to obey were left out?

Helen

But the contract to love — [*To* Theodore.] that's so much worse, it seems to me. Obedience is a mere matter of will, is it not? But when a man promises to love until death ——

"And So They Were Married"

Theodore

Are you so cold, so scientific, so *unsexed*, that you cannot trust the man you love?

Helen

Why, Theodore, if I didn't trust him I'd *marry* him! Contracts are not for those who trust — they're for those who don't.

Lucy

[*takes* Helen *apart*]

Now, I may be old-fashioned, Helen, but I'm a married woman, and I know men. You never can tell, my dear, you never can tell.

Helen

Do you think I'd live with a man who did not love me? Do you think I'd live *on* a man I did not love? [Lucy *blinks.*] Why, what kind of a woman should I be then! The name wife — would that change it? Calling it holy — would that hallow it? ... Every woman, married or not, knows the truth about this! In her soul woman has always known. But until to-day has never dared to tell.

"And So They Were Married"

Ernest
[*approaching* Helen]

Oh, come now — those vows — they aren't intended in a literal sense. Ask Theodore. Why, no sane person means half of that gibgerish. "With all my worldly goods I thee endow" — millions of men have said it — how many ever did it? How many clergymen ever expect them to! . . . It's all a polite fiction in beautiful, sonorous English.

Helen

The most sacred relationship in life! Ernest, shall you and I enter it unadvisedly, lightly, and with LIES on our lips? . . . Simply because others do?

Ernest
[*a little impatient*]

But the whole world stands for this. And the world won't stand for that.

Helen

Is that reverently, soberly, and in the fear of God? No, cynically, selfishly, and in the fear of man. I don't want to be obstinate, I don't like to set myself up as "holier than thou," but, Ernest, unless we begin honestly, we'll end dishonestly. Somehow marriage seems wicked to me.

JUDGE
[*nudging* THEODORE]

How do you like that?

THEODORE

John is right — they've gone mad.

ERNEST

All the same, you've got to marry me — you've simply *got* to.

HELEN

You are mistaken. I do *not* have to marry any one. I can support myself.

ERNEST

Then I'm disappointed in you.

HELEN

And I in you.

ERNEST

I thought you were sensible.

"And So They Were Married"

Helen

I thought you were honest.

Ernest

Honest! You accuse me of dishonesty?

Helen

You don't believe in "half of that gibberish." Yet you are willing to work the Church for our own worldly advantage! You are willing to prostitute the most sacred thing in life! . . . If that is not dishonest, what is!

Ernest

And you are the woman I love and want to marry! In all my life I was never accused of dishonesty before.

Helen

You never tried to marry before. No one is honest about marriage.

Ernest

I never shall try again. I'm going to Paris to-morrow and I'm going alone.

Helen

Then do it. Don't threaten it so often — do it.

"And So They Were Married"

Ernest
I shall. And I'll never come back.

Helen
Nobody asked you to.

Ernest
Helen — for the last time — just for my sake — marry me.

Helen
For the last time — no! no! NO!! I won't be a hypocrite even for your sake.
> [*She turns away, he starts off, then stops, rushes over to her.*

Ernest
> [*holds out arms*]

I can't. You know it. Without you I'm nothing.

Helen
> [*taking both his hands*]

Without you. . . . Oh, my dear, my dear.

Ernest
Forgive me, forgive me.

"And So They Were Married"

Helen

It was all my fault.

Ernest

No, I was a brute. I'm not worthy of you.

Helen

[*covering his lips with her hand*]

Sssh — I can't stand it — I was perfectly horrid to you. And you were doing it all for my sake. [*Laughing and crying.*] You dear old thing — I knew it all the time.

[*They seem about to embrace.*

Judge

[*shaking with laughter*]

Was there ever in the world anything like it! . . . Well, children, see here. He's willing to lie for your sake. She's willing to die for your sake. Now, why not just split the difference and have a civil ceremony for *our* sake.

Theodore

No, they will marry for a better reason. Think of the *sin* of it! [*To* Helen.] Have you no sense of sin?

"And So They Were Married"

Judge

If not, think of the humor of it! Have you no sense of humor?

Helen

[*still drying eyes and smiling to* Judge]

Not a scrap. Neither has Ernest. Have you, dear?

Ernest

I *hope* not — judging from those who always say they have.

Theodore

[*solemnly*]

Helen, look at Ernest — Ernest look at Helen. [*The lovers do so.*] Look into each other's very souls! . . . You know, you *must* know, that in the eyes of God this thing would be a sin, a heinous sin.

[*The lovers gaze deep into each other's eyes in silence.*

Ernest

[*tremulous from the emotion he has just been through*]

The glory and the gladness I see in this woman's eyes a sin? Her trust in me, my worship of her, our new-found belief in a future life,

"And So They Were Married"

our greater usefulness together in this — bah! don't talk to me about sin! Such women cannot sin — they love.

John
[*tired out*]

Oh, you can talk all night, but this is a practical world. How long could you keep your job in the institute? Then how'll you live! Private practice? No respectable home will let you inside the door.

Ernest

I've seen the inside of respectable homes. I want no more. [*Taking from his pocket a piece of paper.*] This morning I came to ask for your sister's hand in marriage. Your manners did not please me. So I cabled over to Metchnikoff. [*Hands cablegram to* John.] His answer. Positions await us both at the Pasteur Institute in Paris. That luxurious suite on to-morrow's steamer still waits in my name.

Theodore

Ernest! Stop! Think! This woman's soul is in your hands.

> [Ernest *seems to hesitate.* Helen *crosses to him.* Judge *seizes* John, *whispers, and shoves him across.*

"And So They Were Married"

John

Doctor Hamilton! I apologize! . . . You're a man of the world. You know what this means — she doesn't. She is in your power — for God's sake go to Paris without her.

[JOHN *tries to lead* HELEN *away from* ERNEST. *She shudders at* JOHN'S *masterful touch and clings to her lover.*

Ernest

And leave her here in *your* power? Never again! You've forced her out of her work — you'd force her into legalized prostitution, if you could, like her innocent little sister. [*Snatches* HELEN *away from* JOHN.] No, married or not, she sails with me in the morning. That's final.

[*The lovers turn away together.*

Judge

Where are you going?

Helen

To ask Marie to pack my trunk.

Ernest

To telephone for a motor.

"And So They Were Married"

JUDGE

But you won't start until after the family party?

ERNEST

Of course not.

[*In a sudden silence* HELEN *and* ERNEST *walk into the house, leaving the family in despair.*

JUDGE
[*after a long sigh, to* JOHN]

I knew you'd bungle it, I knew it — but there's still a chance, just one more card to play. [*The* BUTLER *comes out.*

LUCY

Good heavens! Already?

BUTLER

Mr. and Mrs. Willoughby, Doctor and Mrs. Grey, and the Misses Grey.

LUCY
[*flurried*]

And we're not even dressed!

"And So They Were Married"

Judge

No matter. It's Sunday — many orthodox people . . . why, Mr. Baker won't even dine out on Sunday.

> [*Enter the persons announced. Greetings. "How warm it is for September." . . . "And how's the baby, Margaret?" etc.* John *and* Judge *apart are planning excitedly.* Jean *and* Rex *come out, and finally* Helen, *followed by* Ernest.

Butler

Dinner is served, ma'am.

> [*The* Second Man *touches button. Japanese lanterns glow, silver shines, and all move toward the tables, a happy, united family.*

Lucy

[*going-to-dinner manner as she leads the way*]

We can hardly go out formally because we're already out, you know. Aunt Susan, will you sit over there on John's right? Doctor Hamilton by me? Rex on the other side?

John

Here, Helen. No, Jean, you are beside Rex, you know.

"And So They Were Married"

Judge
Until married, then you're separated.

Lucy
Cousin Charlie — that's it. [*All take their places.*] Most extraordinary weather for September, isn't it?

Judge
[*he slaps his cheek*]

Isn't it?

Lucy
[*shocked and hurt*]

That's the first mosquito I have ever known on our place.

John
[*indignantly*]

We never have mosquitoes here. You must have been mistaken.

> [*The servants are passing in and out of house with courses. The* Butler *now brings a telegram to* Judge.]

Judge
From Julia! [*Tears it open eagerly, reads, and*

"And So They Were Married"

then shouts.] She's coming back to me, she's coming back! Look at that, look at that!

> [*Jumps up and shows telegram to* JOHN. *Then taking it around to* LUCY *he sings to tune of "Merrily we roll along"*:

>> Aunt Julia is coming back
>> Coming back — coming back
>> Aunt Julia is coming back
>> Coming back from Reno.

HELEN
[*laughing*]

From Reno? That sounds like divorce, Uncle Everett.

JUDGE

Like divorce? Does *that* sound like divorce? [*Takes telegram from* LUCY *and hands it to* HELEN.] Read it aloud.

HELEN
[*reading*]

"Dear boy, I can't stand it, either. Come to me or I go to you."

JUDGE
[*sings during the reading*]

Coming back from Reno. [*Breaks off — to*

"And So They Were Married"

HELEN.] So you thought we wanted a divorce, did you?

HELEN

I never dreamed of such a thing.

JUDGE

[*looks at her a moment, then in a burst*]

Well, *I* did. The dream of my life — your Aunt Julia's, too. We thought we believed in trial marriage, but we don't — we believe in trial *separation!*

THEODORE

[*uncomfortably*]

They thought they didn't love each other, but they do, you see.

JUDGE

We don't, we don't, but we can't get along without each other . . . got the habit of having each other around and can't break it. . . . This morning I telegraphed: "Are you doing this just for my sake?" She replied, "Tutti-frutti." [*Sings.*] Aunt Julia's coming back. Oh, I'm too happy to eat. [*Singing, while others eat and drink:*

"And So They Were Married"

Coming back, coming back,
Aunt Julia is coming back
Coming back from Reno.

And I don't care who knows it. The more the better for marriage. The truth — give me more truth, give me more — champagne. [BUTLER *fills glass as* JUDGE *raises it.*] Here's to your Aunt Julia, the best wife — I ever had. [*All rise, drink, laugh, and sit down.*] And I'll never, never get another. . . . You know I thought maybe I might. Oh, Everett, Everett, you sly dog, you old idiot you!

JOHN
[*arises, clearing throat, tapping on glasses for silence*]

And now, speaking of divorce, I have an engagement to announce. [*Some laughter but all quiet down. He smiles at* JEAN.] Of course, you can't guess whose. Friends, it is my privilege to announce the engagement of my good friend Rex Baker to my dear sister Jean. [*Gentle applause and congratulations. Music begins.*] And so I will now ask all to arise and drink to the health and prosperity of my little sister and my brother-in-law to be! And my best wish is that

"And So They Were Married"

they will be as happy as my better half and me. [*All cheer and drink health standing.*] Speech, Rex!

    [*Some of them playfully try to put him on his feet.*]

Rex
[*shaking his head and maintaining his seat*]

I can't make a speech. I'm too happy for words — See-what-I-mean?

Helen
[*in a low, significant tone*]

Jean, aren't you going to say something?

Jean
[*arises, all silent, she looks at* Lucy, Rex, John]

Words cannot describe my happiness, either.

    [*She resumes her seat, and all gather round to congratulate* Jean *and* Rex.

John
[*rapping for quiet*]

One moment, one moment. Another toast, another toast! [*Others quiet down.*] We have with us to-night one who, in honoring whom we

"And So They Were Married"

honor ourselves, one who with capital back of him would soon become the greatest scientist in America! [JUDGE *leads applause,* "hear, hear!" *etc.* JOHN *raises glass.*] To the distinguished guest whom I am proud to welcome to my humble board, to the noble humanitarian whom Mr. Baker delights to honor, to the good friend whom we all admire and trust, Doctor Ernest Hamilton!

[*All applaud and about to drink health,* JUDGE *jumps up.*

JUDGE

And to his fair collaborator! the brave woman who at this modern warrior's side daily risks her life for others, handling death and disease in those mighty but unsung battles for the common weal! [*Applause.*] A New Woman? No, friends, look behind the stupid names the mob would cast, like stones to destroy, look and you will see your true conservative — willing to appear radical in order to conserve woman's work in the world! willing to appear ridiculous to right ancient wrongs! willing even to appear *wrong* — for those she loves! Ah, the same old-fashioned woman we all adore, in a form so new we blindly fail to understand her glorious

"And So They Were Married"

advent before our very eyes! To Helen, the gracious embodiment of all that is sweetest, noblest, and best in womanhood — to Helen! Our lovely Helen!

John
[*up again at once*]

Family approval, social esteem, and an honored career — all this is theirs for the asking! To-day to me they have confessed their love — to-night to you I now announce . . . their engagement! Long life and happiness to Helen and Ernest!

[*Great enthusiasm — even pounding on the table.* Ernest *arises, looking surprised.* John *signalling to rest of family to join in.*

The Family
[*glasses raised, drowning out* Ernest]

Long life and happiness, long life and happiness!

Ernest
[*raises hand*]

Wait! Before you drink this toast. . . . [*The glasses stop midway. Sudden silence.*] Your congratulations we appreciate, your kind wishes

"And So They Were Married"

we desire — but not on false pretences. We are not engaged to be married.

[*In the tense silence a shudder ripples the family joy.*

Rex
[*apart to* Jean]

Gee! They had a scrap, too?

John
[*up, nervously.* Ernest *still standing*]

If I may interrupt. . . . He has financial reasons — I respect him for it. But this very day the Baker Institute in recognition of Doctor Hamilton's distinguished services to humanity has doubled his salary — doubled it! It's all right now — it's all right.

Rex
[*apart to* Jean]

Four thousand, eh? . . . get a very decent touring car for that.

Ernest
[*to all*]

That is very kind, but that is not the point. True, our mutual needs are such that we can-

"And So They Were Married"

not live nor work apart, but our convictions are such that we cannot live and work *together* — in what you have the humor to call "holy wedlock." Now, Helen, the motor is waiting.

[*Sensation. Gasps of amazement and horror. Some jump up from table. A chair is upset.* Ernest *holds* Helen's *wrap. General movement and murmurs.*

John
[*barring way*]

You leave this house only over my dead body.

[*Others gather around lovers.*

Judge
[*to all*]

Stand back! . . . Let him among you who has a purer ideal of love, a higher conception of duty cast the first stone.   [*All stop. Silenced.*

Theodore

But this man and this woman would destroy marriage!

Judge
[*standing beside lovers*]

No! Such as they will not destroy marriage — they will save it! They restore the vital sub-

"And So They Were Married"

stance while we preserve the empty shell. Everything they have said, everything they have done, proves it. The promise to love — they could not help it — they took it — I heard them. The instinct for secrecy — they felt it — we all do — but straightway they told the next of kin. [*Points to* JOHN.] Even when insulted and driven forth from the tribe, they indignantly refused to be driven into each other's arms until you of the same blood could hear them plight their troth! Believe in marriage? Why, there never was, there never will be a more perfect tribute to true marriage than from this fearless pair you now accuse of seeking to destroy it! [JOHN *tries to interrupt, but the* JUDGE *waves him down.*] They have been not only honorable but old-fashioned, save in the one orthodox detail of accepting the authority constituted by society for *its* protection and for *theirs*. [*To* HELEN *and* ERNEST.] But now, I'm sure, before starting on their wedding journey — another old-fashioned convention they believe in — that, just to please us if not themselves, they will consent to be united in the bonds of holy wedlock by Cousin Theodore who stands ready and waiting with prayer-book in hand.

[*Family subsides. Everybody happy.* THEODORE *steps up, opens prayer-book.*

"And So They Were Married"

Theodore

"Dearly beloved, we are gathered together here in the sight of God ——"

Helen
[*suddenly loud and clear*]

Theodore! are you going to marry Rex and Jean?

John
[*impatiently*]

Of course, of course, Mr. Baker's chaplain.

Ernest
[*recoiling*]

Theodore! You! Are you going to stand up and tell the world that God has joined those two together — God?

[Theodore *looks at* John *but does not deny it and says nothing.*

Helen

Then you will be blaspheming love — and God who made it. No, you shall not marry us.

Ernest
[*agreeing with* Helen]

Some things are too sacred to be profaned.

"And So They Were Married"

THEODORE
[*overwhelmed*]
Profaned? ... By the Church?

JOHN
Your love too sacred for the Church? The Church has a name for such love! The world a name for such women!

ERNEST
[*about to strike* JOHN, *then shrugs*]
A rotten world! A kept Church! Come, let's get away from it all! Come!
[HELEN *offers her hand in farewell to* LUCY, *but* JOHN *shields her from* HELEN'S *touch, then to* JEAN. REX *shields* JEAN *from contamination, but* JEAN *weeps.*

JUDGE
[*barring the way. To* ERNEST]
Stop! You cannot! The very tie that binds you to this woman binds you to us and to the whole world with hooks of steel! [*The lovers are still going,* JUDGE *ascends steps, facing them.*] For the last time! before too late! ERNEST! You *know* that in the eyes of God you *are* taking this woman to be your wife.

"And So They Were Married"

Ernest

In the eyes of *God*, I *do* take Helen to be my wife — but ——

Judge

You, Helen! Speak, woman, speak!

Helen

I take Ernest to be my husband in the eyes of God, but ——

Judge

[*raises his hand augustly and in a voice of authority*]

Then, since you, Ernest, and you, Helen, have made this solemn declaration before God and in the presence of witnesses, I, by the authority vested in me by the laws of this State do now pronounce you man and wife!

> [Mr. *and* Mrs. Hamilton *look at each other bewildered. Meanwhile the silence has been pierced, first by a little hysterical scream from* Jean, *then the others all wake up and crowd about the happy pair, congratulating them. The women who had snubbed* Helen *before cover her with kisses, for now she is fit for their embraces.*

"And So They Were Married"

John
[*to* Theodore]

Saved! Saved! Respectable at last, thank God. [*Raising his glass and hammering for attention.*] Here's to the bride and groom.

[All *cheer, raise glasses, and drink.*

Ernest
[*when the noise dies down. As the others kiss* Helen]

A moment ago you were a bad woman. Now [*to all*] behold! she is a good woman. Marriage is wonderful.

[John *and* Lucy *run to* Judge *and shake hands.*

Judge
[*to* John *and* Lucy, *his wife*]

Yes, Respectability has triumphed this time, but let Society take warning and beware! beware! beware!

Curtain